Corey Pavin's
SHOTMAKING

with Guy Yocom

GOLF
DIGEST

POCKET BOOKS

New York   London
Toronto   Sydney
Tokyo   Singapore

Published by:

NYT Special Services, Inc.
A Subsidiary of the New York Times Company Magazine Group,Inc.
5520 Park Avenue, Box 395
Trumbull, CT 06611-0395

and

POCKET BOOKS, a division of Simon & Schuster Inc.
1230 Avenue of the Americas, New York, NY 10020

ISBN: 0-671-54513-2

First NYT Special Services, Inc. and Pocket Books trade paperback printing June 1997

10 9 8 7 6 5 4 3 2 1

COVER DESIGN BY ROD HERNANDEZ
FRONT PHOTO BY SZURLEJ / *THE NEW YORK TIMES*

BOOK DESIGN BY LAURA HAMMOND HOUGH

Printed in the U.S.A.

To Shannon, for always being there for me. All her support has enabled me to become a better golfer and, more importantly, a better person. Having her on my side has made all the difference. And to Ryan and Austin, whose presence in our lives has inspired us both to enjoy life more and be good parents.

I dedicate my life to Jesus Christ. Wonderful things have happened since He entered my life.

> "And we rejoice in the hope of the glory of God.
>
> "Not only so, but we also rejoice in our sufferings, because we know that suffering produces perseverance; perseverance, character; and character, hope. And hope does not disappoint us, because God has poured out his love into our hearts by the Holy Spirit, who he has given us.
>
> "You see, at just the right time, when we were still powerless, Christ died for the ungodly. Very rarely will anyone die for a righteous man, though for a good man someone might possibly dare to die. But God demonstrates his own love for us in this: While we were still sinners, Christ died for us."
>
> —ROMANS 5:2B-8

ACKNOWLEDGMENTS

MY PARENTS, JACK AND BARBARA PAVIN, gave me the opportunity to start playing golf. I'll always be grateful.

My older brothers, Matt and Fletcher, used to let me play along with them when we were young. Those early rounds at Las Posas Country Club gave me a sound start.

I want to extend my appreciation to instructor Chuck Cook of Austin, Texas, for the swing help he gave me prior to my winning the 1995 U.S. Open. Thanks also to instructor Bruce Hamilton for his 20 years of molding my swing.

Sports psychologist Dr. Richard Coop provided invaluable help with my mental approach to the game. He taught me how to channel my energy in positive directions. There is more to the game than swinging a club, and he helped make the game fun for me again.

I also want to thank Chris Noss, my personal trainer. He motivated me to work hard at improving my physical fitness.

CONTENTS

FOREWORD

by Tom Watson

WHEN I THINK OF COREY PAVIN'S GOLF SWING I always think of the PGA Tour's great Irish humorist, David Feherty, who once likened Corey's swing to "an octopus falling out of a tree."

Now, one may think this is a somewhat odd or even cold-hearted opening thought for someone who is writing a foreword to a friend's instructional golf book. But I stand by it—at least when I observe his *practice swing*. When it's time to put the clubface on the ball, Corey has one of the truest swings in golf today.

Although Corey isn't blessed with the great strength of a John Daly or Ernie Els (Corey ranked 159th in driving distance in 1995), he has learned and perfected the true meaning of the game, which was simply stated to me by one of my many teachers, Herman Scharlan. Along with such truisms as "nothing rolls like a ball" and "the flight of the ball never lies," Herman stated there are only four ways you can flight the ball: high, low, left-to-right and right-to-left. If a golfer can learn those four ways of flighting the ball, then he or she will be called a shotmaker and will certainly be the envy of those one-trick ponies who have only one shot they can rely on under pressure.

Foreword

Corey Pavin is to be envied as a shotmaker. But shotmakers alone do not become champions. Champions must have a high degree of talent, but most importantly, they must have heart. Sam Snead once said he'd take as a partner any player composed of "50 percent talent and 100 percent heart" over a player who was "50 percent heart and 100 percent talent" every time. There is no one in golf today who has more heart or this "never say die" attitude than Corey.

Here are a few examples of Corey's exceptional talent and his "blood and guts" attitude:

- On the 72nd hole during the 1992 Honda Classic played at Weston Hills Country Club in Florida, Corey holed his 8-iron third shot for an eagle 3 to propel him into a playoff against Fred Couples, which Corey won.
- In a fierce singles match during the final day of the 1991 Ryder Cup at Kiawah Island, S.C., Corey, using a sand wedge, blasted his ball from a plugged downhill lie in a sand dune to within three feet of the cup to preserve a crucial victory against Steven Richardson of the European team. The U.S. won that Ryder Cup by one point.
- On the second day of the 1995 Ryder Cup Matches, Corey and his four-ball partner, Loren Roberts, arrived at the final hole of the last match all square against Nick Faldo and Bernhard Langer. Corey faced a treacherous downhill chip and he stoically holed the shot for a birdie 3 to win the match, putting the U.S. team two points ahead of the European team with 12 singles matches yet to play. That stunning chip was a portent of a U.S. victory, but the Europeans won the next day after staging a terrific comeback.
- Finally, there was The Shot. On the 72nd hole of the 1995 U.S. Open at Shinnecock Hills Golf Club, Corey's running (in more ways than one!) 4-wood shot stopped four feet from the cup and secured his first major championship victory. It will undoubtedly be remembered as one of the greatest pressure shots in golf history.

During his career Corey has demonstrated the uncanny ability time and again to, in Harvey Penick's words, "take dead aim" at the flagstick and succeed.

What is Corey's secret?

There *is* no secret.

There is simply his true understanding of how to flight the ball and the guts to pull off creative shots under the most extreme pressure.

Sit back, learn and enjoy the words from a man who helped define the term, "gut check."

Introduction

SHOTMAKING: PART SCIENCE, PART ART

IF CONDITIONS ARE JUST RIGHT, I can pump my drives out there pretty far. Give me a dry, firm fairway, and I have a specialty shot, a low draw, that runs forever. Never mind that I ranked 159th in driving distance on the PGA Tour in 1995. On hard ground, I'm sneaky long.

If the fairways are wet, though, forget it. By PGA Tour standards, I'm a short hitter. For me to get a lot of distance, I need a dry fairway and lots of roll. I just can't carry the ball as far as some of the big boys.

So do I prefer dry, hard fairways? Not really. I really couldn't care less if the fairways are wet or dry. Distance is only one aspect of the game, one small component of the total makeup of a golfer. The biggest obstacle to playing golf well has little to do with how far you hit the ball, nor does it have much to do with your strength or talent level. My appearance has never scared anybody. I'm 5-foot-9 and weigh 150 pounds. I wasn't blessed with great natural strength. I'm a fair natural athlete but not an exceptional one. How did I succeed?

The problem amateurs have—and I see it every week in pro-ams—is that they basically have only one shot in their bags. They hit the ball far enough, own the latest in equipment and play often enough. But they only have one shot they can count on, and that means trouble.

Introduction

More times during a round than you realize, you face a situation where the course is telling you what type of shot to play, but you don't have full command of that shot and are reluctant to play it. If you're driving on a hole where the fairway bends from right to left and your natural shot is a left-to-right fade, an uncomfortable feeling sets in. If you "play it safe" and hit that natural fade anyway, you'll be penalized regardless of the outcome. That perfect fade in the fairway isn't necessarily productive because the ball will curve away from the hole, and you'll face a long second shot. If you fade the ball too much, you'll be in trouble on the right. And if (heaven forbid) you try to draw the ball, it will be like playing the lottery. How often do you win the lottery?

Lack of versatility in the ways you can work the ball is a killer. On the other hand, even a short hitter can play great golf if he can hit the shot that's required. That same right-to-left driving hole isn't so imposing to the golfer who can shape a shot right to left. The player who can hit a low shot into the wind is much better off than the big bruiser who has only the high, towering shot at his command.

I grew up playing at Las Posas Country Club in Camarillo, California. It was a short course, only 6,300 yards, and par was 71. Yet it demanded that I develop all types of shots to play it well. Las Posas is hilly, treelined and had lots of dogleg holes. Out-of-bounds stakes flanked both sides of the fairways on almost every hole, and from stake to stake there was a distance of only 50 yards. A breeze seemed to blow constantly. As I grew older and hit the ball far enough to reach the corners of the doglegs, I was forced to develop draws and fades to fit the natural contours and designs. In short, it was a shotmaker's course, and it helped make me the player I am today.

As a kid, I didn't pick out one PGA Tour pro as a hero. I wanted to develop a game that was well-rounded and complete. So I cherry-picked individual players who were great in a specific area of the game.

For consistency, the ability to play well day in and day out, I wanted to be Tom Kite. For course management, the capacity to play each hole strategically, I chose Jack Nicklaus. (I wanted Jack's power, too, but knew I'd never have it.) I wanted Tom Watson's chipping ability and his putter, too—when I was 13, Tom was the best putter in the game.

These fellows combined would have made the perfect golfer. But after I turned pro, I came to admire several other players who were difficult to categorize. I loved the way Hale Irwin hit wonderfully creative shots even from the middle of the fairway, bending the ball this way and that, using three-quarter swings and making the ball behave so it would snuggle up close to the hole. Lanny Wadkins fell into that category, too. Then there was Seve Ballesteros, the all-time artist *extraordinaire.*

Hale, Lanny and Seve proved to me that golf really is two games. There's the mechanical end of it, the science of swinging the club correctly, powerfully and efficiently. Then there's the side that can best be described as an art. Golf would be pretty boring if we were robots and merely programmed ourselves to hit one perfect shot after another. But the game requires you to use your imagination, too. Radically different hole designs, the variety of lies you get, the wind, the grasses you play off of, different weather conditions, they all demand flexibility in our thinking, our approach, and the way we play golf shots. The same course changes every day, and so does the golfer. All of these variables make golf a better, more fascinating, game. They heighten our enjoyment and keep the challenge intact.

Shotmaking falls under the "art" category. Good shotmaking requires good mechanics, but it calls for much more than that. Shotmaking is the ability to create a shot in your mind's eye that fits the demands of the hole you're playing, and to play that shot with confidence. Shotmaking is the ability to deviate from your trusted, bread-and-butter shot and create one more aptly suited to the conditions. Shotmaking is hitting quality shots from poor lies and feeling immense satisfaction when the shot comes off as planned.

In a sense, shotmaking sets you free. It atones for your physical limitations, eradicates the fear of playing certain holes and increases the number of possibilities you have every time you step up to the ball. It gives you the freedom to be aggressive on full shots into the green, for good shotmaking skills around the green enable you to get the ball up and down if you hit a poor shot. Shotmaking sets you free in a literal sense, too—only by being a good shotmaker can you escape from trouble effectively.

Introduction

I may tend to glamorize shotmaking, but I don't want to belittle sound fundamentals. In fact, the cornerstone of good shotmaking is good mechanics. Only with a dependable, sound, repeating swing—and a clear understanding of the principles behind it—can you make the necessary adjustments that produce creative golf shots.

In structuring the hard-core instruction parts of this book, I'll begin by explaining the basic fundamentals of your grip, setup and swing. I'll explain the laws of ball flight. Then I'll explain in detail how to create shots with every club in your bag, including the putter. I'll discuss strategy, club selection, trouble shots and how to get in the right frame of mind to hit difficult shots in competitive situations.

But first, I want to recount four very interesting days at a place called Shinnecock Hills Golf Club. I was at my shotmaking best, and you might be able to learn something from my experience there.

COREY PAVIN
January 1996

Chapter 1

REVISITING THE
1995 U.S. OPEN

I **DON'T LIKE TO LOSE** playoffs. The satisfaction I get from finishing second never overrides the disappointment of not winning the whole thing. But when I lost to Lee Janzen in a sudden-death playoff at the Kemper Open early last June, I left the TPC at Avenel in Maryland feeling less despondent than usual. After Lee made his putt to beat me, I walked over to congratulate him. Before I could say anything, Lee spoke first.

"The guy who finishes second the week before the U.S. Open, wins the Open," he said.

That made me laugh. "You're just trying to make me feel good," I said.

But I *had* played well, and the U.S. Open the following week was to be played at Shinnecock Hills Golf Club in Southampton, N.Y., a real shotmaker's course. I had just changed putters, I had excellent control of my game and my attitude was good. There was every reason to be optimistic. I arrived there with an open mind, and I was determined. I had been a pro for 13 years and had not yet won a major championship. The press was referring to me as "the best player who hasn't won a major," a sort of backhanded compliment that didn't bother me as much as it might have bothered some other players. What bothered me was that I felt my golf game was good enough to produce a major victory, and I hadn't won one yet. It was a personal thing.

Shinnecock Hills is one of the greatest courses in the world. My memories of the course were vague and not altogether good because the first time I saw it, during the 1986 U.S. Open, I played lousy and missed the cut. My first son, Ryan, had been born only two weeks before, and my mind was with Shannon, my wife, and our new baby.

When I played my first practice round at Shinnecock last year, it was like seeing the course for the first time. I was in awe. It has no weak holes, unlike most other "great" courses. I have a habit of redesigning holes in my mind as I play them, and rarely do I play a course that is so balanced, so flowing from start to finish, that I can't think of at least a few subtle changes. But at Shinnecock, every hole is strong. It has tremendous balance and variety. It demands that you shape a lot of shots. You have to curve the ball both ways, hit it high and low, lob the ball and spin it. Almost every green has an opening in the front, so you have the choice of bouncing it in there or flying it on the green. And it is beautiful to look at.

Then there are the conditions. The wind blows constantly, usually pretty hard. It doesn't always blow from the same direction, either. The U.S. Golf Association set up the course to play very difficult. If you missed the fairway at all, you were in trouble. And if you missed the fairway by a lot, you were in *serious* trouble. The knee-high grass the TV announcers kept referring to as "native fescue" was brutal. Hit it there and usually you just had to wedge it back to the fairway.

Still, the course suited me perfectly. The USGA hadn't grown the rough around the greens to a ridiculous degree, and that would work to my advantage. My shotmaking skill around the greens is one of my strengths and when the grass is short you have more shot options to choose from.

My strategy for Shinnecock was the same as for any U.S. Open: Hit the fairways, hit the greens and take what the course would give me. I knew better than to be overly aggressive because the course was just too punishing and unrelenting. A careless shot could mean a double bogey or worse. I felt I had to play smart, pick my spots. If I had a clean opportunity to hit it close with 8- or 9-iron or wedge, fine. Most of the time, however, I wanted to play for the part of the green that would give me an easy two-putt, or at worst a serviceable opportunity to get the ball up and down if I missed the green. And I *would* miss greens. We all would.

The tournament finally got under way. And armed with my fool-proof strategy, I promptly bogeyed the first hole. Another bogey followed. Through four holes I was two over par.

Then, on the fifth hole, a long par 5, I holed a 115-yard 9-iron third shot for an eagle 3. It was your basic omen that this might not be such a bad day after all. I struggled after that, hitting the ball poorly but getting up and down for pars several times. I came in with a two-over-par 72 and headed for the practice range. The session I spent there led to an adjustment in my backswing that won me the championship three days later.

I played better the second day. The key was the 18th hole, a 450-yard par 4 that extends straight out from the tee and then sweeps uphill and to the left toward an elusive green protected by bunkers and tall grass. My tee shot left me with roughly 220 yards to the hole. I chose a 4-wood and played one of my best shots of the tournament, a low, penetrating draw that stopped 10 feet from the hole. I came in with a 69.

By Saturday, the day of the third round, I had my game going and had climbed into contention for the lead. On the 18th, I hit a poor drive to the left into that native fescue and played a sand wedge to the fairway about 90 yards from the green. I sure didn't want to end the day with a bogey, and I used the same sand wedge to hit the ball five feet from the hole. I saved my par and, by coming in with a score of 71, was only three strokes out of the lead. Only four players were ahead of me and I was only two over par for the tournament. I was right in the thick of it.

The day ended on a strange note. After I signed my scorecard, no one asked me to go to the media room for an interview. None of the reporters were interested in talking with me except for Roger Maltbie of NBC. And even Roger wasn't asked to interview me until minutes before I teed off in the final round. I didn't have the distraction of having the media surrounding me, which was fine because it can make the pressure a little more intense. But at the same time, I was thinking, "Why aren't they paying any attention to me?" I couldn't help but think they didn't consider me a threat to win, and I left the course feeling motivated to prove them wrong.

The final day of a major can be intense and stressful, but for some reason I felt fine. In fact I felt *better* than fine. Part of the reason was because it was Father's Day, and Shannon, Ryan and Austin had given me a great Father's Day morning. I felt a strange mixture of calmness, intensity, relaxation and focus that is difficult to describe. For all of the pressure, I felt like I was about to play a practice round. It was eerie, really, a state of mind where everything is breathtakingly clear and you perform effortlessly without much conscious thought. It's called The Zone, and I was in it.

I parred the first hole. At the second, a long par 3, I missed the green and hit my chip too hard. It was really humming across the green, straight on line but with enough speed to go seven or eight feet past the hole. Then, *bam.* The ball struck the flagstick squarely and stopped a foot away. A tap-in par and a great break. It gave me a lot of confidence.

I had so much confidence, in fact, that I wasn't upset when I bogeyed the next hole, my only bogey of the day. I was three over par for the tournament now, four strokes behind the leaders but not particularly worried because the wind was picking up and there was a lot of golf yet to be played. I was far from out of it.

I made a tough seven-foot putt for par at the seventh. At the ninth I hit a 6-iron seven feet behind the hole, leaving a putt that was so quick I only had to touch the ball to get it to the hole. I hit the ball just hard enough to get it rolling, and it trickled right into the middle of the cup for a birdie. I was back to two over for the tournament and I couldn't help but glance at the leader board. *Voila,* nobody was under par. I was only two shots back.

I parred 10 and 11, and at 12 I hit a good iron shot to about 12 feet. The putt was straight uphill with a right-to-left break, the kind of putt I like. My only thought was to hit the putt firmly and positively, to give it a chance to go in. I rapped the putt and it went right in the back of the hole. Now I was only one over par, and there was no doubt that the leaders, playing behind me, had to know what I was up to. I parred the next two holes. Then, while I was standing on the 15th tee waiting to hit, I watched Greg Norman bogey to go one over, while Tom Lehman birdied to also go to one over. I was tied for the lead!

Adrenaline was pumping through me. At 15 I hit the ball 12 feet from the hole, and I nailed the putt dead center. The leader board now confirmed that I had the outright lead in the U.S. Open.

Now I was nervous. I knew that if I birdied one of the last three holes, I probably would win. At 16 my 3-wood second shot left me 110 yards to the hole, dead into the wind. I hit a little 8-iron that landed 15 feet left of the hole and drifted to within 10 feet. I just missed the birdie putt, but as it turned out, par was a good score.

At the 17th, a middle-length par 3, I stood on the tee and tried to figure out how to play one of the hardest shots I've ever seen. The wind was howling from the left, and the pin was on the left side of the green. Compounding the problem was the fact that the green also sloped to the left. It was only a middle-iron shot, but just getting it on the green was a tough challenge.

I chose a 6-iron and hit one of the best shots of the tournament, maybe my life. I aimed at the flagstick and played a right-to-left draw, so the ball would hook into the wind. Because the wind was blowing so hard, I figured it would stop the ball from hooking and keep the shot on line. It came off almost perfectly, the wind sweeping the ball to the back right portion of the green, where it came to rest 40 feet from the hole. In most cases a shot 40 feet from the hole is not that great, but in this case I was thrilled. It was all I could have asked for.

My first putt rolled five feet past the hole. The second putt wasn't easy, and I was feeling more pressure than I had ever felt in my career. But I hit the putt solidly and it tracked right on line into the hole. One more hole, one more par, and the U.S. Open probably was mine.

Then the worst possible thing happened. I came to the 18th tee and endured a 10-minute wait while the players ahead of me cleared the fairway. Remembering the advice of my sports psychologist, Dr. Richard Coop, I did everything I could to get my mind off the drive I had to hit. It does you no good to think about an important shot before the time comes to play it. Negative thoughts will enter your mind and stay there. If you use your "down time" intelligently, you'll be able to focus on the shot and go through your routine without any outside thoughts rattling around in the back of your mind.

So I had some time to kill. I walked over to my playing partner, Ian Woosnam, and asked him when he planned to fly out of New York. Ian said he was leaving that night. A couple of state troopers were standing nearby, and I brought *them* into the conversation, asking what the traffic was going to be like and whether Ian would be able to make his flight.

Finally, it was time for me to hit. I selected a spot about 20 yards beyond the ball as my intermediate target, went through my routine and lost the spot. I started over and got set. The drive was real solid. It went farther to the right than I wanted, but in the previous rounds I had missed my drive to the left twice, and I didn't want to miss it there again. A draw would have gone 35 yards farther than a slight fade, but distance wasn't that important. I had to hit the ball in the fairway. And I did.

When I got to my ball, I found I had 209 yards to the front of the green, 228 to the hole. I started a little discussion with my caddie, Eric Schwarz. I asked him if I could get a 2-iron to the green.

"No, I think it's a 4-wood," Eric said firmly.

I told Eric I agreed with him. I then started planning how to play the shot, speaking my thoughts aloud to affirm to myself that I was thinking clearly. "I'll aim this at the right edge of the green with a little draw and let the wind carry the ball toward the hole."

Eric agreed that definitely was the way to play the shot. By aiming to the right, I took the trouble to the left of the green out of play. So I took the 4-wood, made a few practice swings, addressed the ball and swung. The ball came off low and then started to draw. It swung a fraction to the left and settled on a line to the hole. It landed on a little flat area short of the green, bounced up and rolled toward the hole.

I thought for a minute it might roll into the hole. From my vantage point, all I could see was the ball and the flagstick. I couldn't wait. I started running toward the hole. When I saw the ball was within five feet of the pin, I managed to slow down to a walk.

That walk up the 18th fairway was something. The fans were yelling and I got pretty emotional—fired-up emotional, not weepy emotional. The tournament wasn't over yet. I tried to stay calm but it wasn't easy. I had to collect myself because I knew if I made the putt, I'd win the Open for sure. A par *probably* would win and would at least tie. In any case, I had to block everything out and concentrate on the golf I had left to play.

I read the putt carefully and read the line correctly. I wasn't feeling nervous in any way. I went through my routine. Eric liked the right edge of the cup and I agreed. And I missed the putt badly. The ball didn't touch the hole.

My nervousness returned. Now I had a putt a little over a foot in length, and I'd just pulled my first putt. Everybody's missed a few one-footers in their time. I went through my routine again, got over the putt and knocked it in the hole.

Several minutes later, I had won the U.S. Open. The hours that followed were some of the happiest of my life. Shannon, Ryan and Austin were there, and later on that evening we went up on the club-house roof with Lee Janzen and his wife, Bev, and popped some cham-pagne. Shannon and I had waited a long time for a major cham-pionship, and it turned out to be worth waiting for.

I poured virtually everything I knew and had learned about the game in 25 years into those four days. I had to hit every shot with all the physical, intellectual and emotional resources I had. In this book, I'll impart all I know about shotmaking to you.

I hope it helps and that you enjoy reading it. If you receive half of the satisfaction that comes through improving that I have, the effort will have been worthwhile.

THE PRACTICE DRILL
THAT WON THE U.S. OPEN

Every golfer tends to have an individual swing flaw that surfaces occa-sionally and without warning. No matter how much you practice or how long you play the game, that tendency will keep cropping up. It's wise to know the cause of that flaw and the best cure for it, so you can solve it quickly without too much detective work.

My tendency is to take the club back too far on the outside during the backswing. If I swing down along the same path, the clubhead travels from outside-to-inside and I hit a weak slice down the middle. It's not a strong fade because I'm just holding on to the club to prevent the clubhead from turning over and causing a pull to the left. There's very little power. I hate that shot.

On the other hand, if at the top of the backswing I loop the club to the inside, I tend to loop it *too* far, so my swing path is excessively inside-to-outside. To prevent a duck hook, I instinctively move my body laterally and hit a push to the right. I hate that shot, too.

The key for me, then, is to take the club back to the inside to begin with. A drill I've used since 1990 helps me a lot. I place two clubs

1-1, 1-2: Here's a reprise of the practice drill that straightened me out at the '95 U.S. Open. First, I place two clubs on the ground parallel to each other, one stationed barely outside the ball. To avoid striking the shaft with my clubhead, I'm forced to swing the club back along an inside path. Taking the club too far outside is a common error and a serious one.

on the ground, one along my feet and the other just outside the ball and parallel to the first (*1-1*). With those clubs on the ground, I can't take the club back outside, or the clubhead will strike the club running just outside my ball. I'm forced to start the club back along an inside path (*1-2*). Well into the backswing, the club continues to swing to the inside (*1-3*). At the top (*1-4*), I'm perfectly on plane and have increased the chances of swinging the clubhead into the ball on a path that's dead-on toward the target.

Your problem may be different than mine, but my point is, find an instructor or devise for yourself a drill that will effectively address the flaw you are prone to.

1-3, 1-4: Taking the club back to the inside helps establish an on-plane swing. At the top, I'm in perfect position to swing the club into the ball along an inside path.

1-5, 1-6: The practice swing you see me make on television has a definite pur-
pose. It starts by my taking the clubhead back along an exaggerated inside path,
turning my right shoulder behind me. I then set the club correctly at the top.

ABOUT THAT 'FUNNY'
PRACTICE SWING...

The aspect of my game I've been asked most about is the practice swing I take just before I begin my preshot routine. The TV cameras caught me doing it a lot during the U.S. Open. The practice swing is comprised of my swinging the club back on an exaggerated inside path *(1-5)*, setting the club at the top *(1-6)*, then making a sudden over-the-top move *(1-7)* that makes me swipe across the ball from outside to inside *(1-8)*.

That practice swing is geared toward erasing my old problem of

1-7, 1-8: The downswing portion of my practice swing is an exaggerated over-the-top move in which I move the club through the hitting area on an outside-to-inside swing path. This isn't the type of action I make when I actually hit a shot, unless I'm deliberately playing a huge slice.

taking the club back too far outside. I use it as an on-course version of the practice drill I described earlier. By rehearsing a backswing that is excessively to the inside, I decrease my chances of taking the club back too far outside when I actually play the shot. Moreover, I try to take the club back on the inside by turning my right shoulder behind me, rather than just whipping the club back with my arms and hands.

It looks unorthodox, I know. But it works.

There also is the practice swing I make where I position the club upright, rest my left hand on top of the handle and, leaving my left hand in place, perform a full "backswing" *(1-9, 1-10)*. The object of this

1-9, 1-10: The other type of practice swing I make is performed without a ball. My goal here is to feel my shoulders turning almost parallel with the ground. By ingraining this sensation, I avoid the tendency of tilting my left shoulder downward and swinging too upright.

drill is to encourage a full shoulder turn that is on the correct, flattish plane. If your backswing is too short, all kinds of problems crop up.

REFLECTIONS ON
'THE SHOT'

The 4-wood I hit to the 72nd green at Shinnecock Hills was one of the better shots of my career. I'll describe the strategy behind it in detail here because it illustrates what the process of shotmaking is all about.

First, the conditions. I had 209 yards to the front of the green and

228 yards to the hole. The wind was blowing hard from the right, and the pin was set on the back left quadrant of the green. My lie was good.

I chose the 4-wood, although I briefly considered hitting a hard 2-iron. But a big, aggressive swing is always dangerous when you're trying to hit the ball solidly and work the ball one direction or the other. Under the circumstances I wanted to take a bogey out of the equation and that meant hitting the ball smoothly with the 4-wood. I knew I had plenty of club and that was comforting.

The first task was to take the trouble to the left of the green completely out of play. There was tall grass well to the left, a near impossible place from which to get the ball up and down. Even a miss just off the green would have left a very difficult chip. If I were going to miss the shot, I wanted it to miss to the right, where the conditions were far more forgiving. So I aimed at the right edge of the green and set up to draw the ball slightly. The hook spin would cause the ball to curve to the left, and the wind would blow the ball even farther to the left but not enough to get me in trouble.

Finally, I wanted to hit the ball low to prevent the wind from affecting it as much. This shot would give me more control because I could start the ball on line. I also knew a low shot doesn't curve as much as a ball hit high in the air. I didn't want a high, sweeping trajectory on this shot.

I played the ball back in my stance to promote the low shot.

I aligned my feet on a line toward the middle of the green, which meant that my target line was to the right half of the green.

I turned my right foot out slightly to promote a full turn on my backswing. My left foot was perpendicular to the target line.

I aimed the clubface slightly to the left of the target line to promote a draw.

By the time I set myself over the ball, there were three possible outcomes for the shot, all of them good. If I failed to draw the ball and hit it straight, I'd hit the ball on the right half of the green and more than likely two-putt for par. If I blocked the shot to the right, I would leave myself a fairly simple chip. And if the shot came off exactly as I planned, the ball would draw toward the hole.

As luck and a decent swing would have it, the ball came off just as I planned. I stayed down on the shot well after impact and didn't look up until the ball was well on the way to the target. I looked to see the ball turning toward the flagstick.

The rest is history. Now let's explore the elements that went into this shot and every other you'll face in golf.

C h a p t e r   2

SQUARE ONE: FINDING YOUR FUNDAMENTALS

I WISH I COULD SAY I'VE DISCOVERED, once and for all, the secret to playing well every day. That's not the case, of course. Golf is a game of finding it, losing it, then finding it again. I've gone through a slump or two in my time—every professional has—and I suppose in the future I'll experience periods where I'm troubled by some aspect of my game.

The best any golfer can hope for is to build a swing so firmly rooted in the fundamentals that those periods of poor play are shortened in number and duration. In almost every case, bad swing habits can be traced to some breakdown in the basics. *I can't emphasize enough the importance of grip, stance, posture, ball position and the basic mechanics of the swing itself.*

It's not enough to understand how to play different golf shots. You have to grasp *why* the changes you make in your stance, setup and ball position affect the ball's behavior. This knowledge will make your practice much more productive. You'll know for certain whether you're working on the correct swing modification. You'll be able to chart your progress more effectively, and your goal will always stay in focus. Shotmaking embraces the more advanced principles of golf, and before you can master the technical aspects of playing unusual shots, you have to have a firm grasp of the fundamentals.

The basics of a sound setup and swing aren't complicated. They're the same for every golfer. Once you understand those concepts and make them a part of your practice and playing regimen, you can go forward and try out some of the more advanced shotmaking techniques. Good basics make shotmaking so much easier. They simplify your technique enormously because the changes you make to hit specialty shots are basically variations on the same themes.

I should point out that some so-called "fundamentals" aren't fundamentals at all. *True* fundamentals never change regardless of the club you're hitting or the type of shot you're playing. Some factors, such as ball position, are extremely important, but they also vary depending on the club you're using. So ball position doesn't rate as a fundamental.

Here are the true fundamentals. Learn them now and never change them. They're the basics from which everything else trickles down.

1. THE GRIP:
ANYTHING GOES—WITHIN REASON

The grip is the foundation of the golf swing. After all, your hands are the only part of your anatomy in contact with the club. Yet my views on the grip are pretty relaxed. I've seen so many different types of grips used effectively that I'm reluctant to recommend one grip for everyone. Whether you interlock, overlap or use a 10-finger grip is almost irrelevant. I've always used an overlapping grip, with the little finger of my right hand placed between the forefinger and middle finger of my left hand when my grip is complete. But that's just my preference.

The same thing goes for "weak" or "strong" grips. There have been great shotmakers with weak grips and great ones with strong grips. I prefer a fairly weak left-hand grip, with the back of my left hand almost facing the target. Other top players, such as Ben Hogan and Bill Rogers, have also had weak left-hand grips. But there have also been great players with strong left-hand grips—Paul Azinger, Bernhard Langer and Lee Trevino come to mind. Within reason, the way you hold the club is strictly a matter of preference and comfort. I don't buy this business of "seeing three knuckles at address" or any other tenet that tells you exactly how to hold the club.

This isn't to say that the grip should be ignored altogether. All great shotmakers have one factor in common with the way they hold the club: The two hands must work together throughout the golf swing. Position-wise, they must coincide so they act in harmony. If you have a strong right-hand grip, then you must have a strong grip with the left hand, too. If one hand is turned to the left and the other is positioned well to the right, your hands will fight each other during the swing.

A simple procedure will insure that your hands work together as a unit during the swing. First, place your left hand on the handle so it feels comfortable (*2-1*). Now place your right hand on the handle so

2-1—2-3: The left hand should feel comfortable when you place it on the club. For me, that means placing my thumb almost down the center of the grip (left). When you add the right hand, place the lifeline running inside your right palm along the side of your left thumb (center). The completed grip (right) should feel firm and unified so the hands perform as a team.

the lifeline of your right hand is placed alongside the thumb of your left hand (2-2). Now close your right hand. The completed grip (2-3) should feel secure, your two hands behaving as one.

One more detail. The thumb of your left hand should always be placed just to the right of center on the handle of the club. You don't want it resting directly on top of the handle, or at all to the left of center. With the right hand, it's just the opposite. The thumb of your right hand should always rest just to the left of center. This takes the thumb "out of play" during the swing. You don't want the thumb of your right hand controlling the club. It's too strong and too difficult to control.

Your grip should *never* change. It isn't necessary. With the exception of putting, where you're using hardly any hand and wrist action at all, you should use the same grip on all shots. If you need to vary the shape and quality of your shots, you should alter your stance, setup, clubface position and other factors. By changing your grip to suit a specific shot, you complicate the shot enormously. Learn the correct grip, then leave it alone.

2. STANCE IS CRITICAL

Your stance determines alignment—the direction your body is aimed at address. Stance also determines the length and shape of your swing, provides stability and promotes good balance. Yet in my opinion, this fundamental doesn't get the attention it deserves.

Let's start with stance width. The distance you set your feet apart at address helps determine the amount of upper body movement versus movement in the legs and feet. The wider your stance, the more active your upper body is during the swing. I'm a believer in a fairly wide stance. I believe the upper body should be the most active part of your body during the swing.

On all standard shots, I place my feet shoulder-width apart, so if I drew vertical lines running downward from the outside of my shoulders, they would intersect the centers of both feet. This is a shade wider than standard. Early in my career, my stance was narrower, and it encouraged a great deal of superfluous leg action. That in turn led to my hips getting too active. All told, there were too many moving parts in my swing. It made me too inconsistent. Widening my stance, I simplified my swing.

Moreover, a wider stance gives you a much firmer foundation. You should have the feeling of solidity and balance, even when swinging all-out. How do you know when your stance is too wide? If you find that your feet and knees become "stuck," or totally lacking mobility during the swing, you're too wide. I don't advise placing your feet much wider at address than mine are.

Note that stance width is the same for all standard full-swing shots regardless of the club I'm using. On short pitches and chips, you can narrow your stance because you don't need a solid foundation. But on any full shot, be it with a 5-iron or the driver, your stance width doesn't change (2-4, 2-5).

2-4, 2-5: Your stance width shouldn't vary on a full shot, regardless of the club you are using. The fairly wide stance I demonstrate here gives you a combination of mobility and stability.

3. THE FEET AND KNEES

Every athlete, from a shortstop in baseball to a linebacker waiting to react to the snap of a football, flexes the knees at address. This prepares the body to move quickly in any direction. In golf, too, you need to flex your knees slightly at address, just enough so they don't become locked at the joints.

Flexing the knees too much is a serious error. You should never flex them so much that you feel as though you're squatting or sitting down. Too much knee flex encourages you to set your upper body too upright, too perpendicular, to the ground. You can't lean forward from the hips properly, and your backswing will be a mess. Bend at your knees just enough to remove tension from the knee joints *(2-6)*.

The position of your feet at address is important, too, because it determines the length of your backswing and your ability to maintain

2-6: Flexing the knees ever so slightly allows freedom and agility, not just in your legs but in your upper body as well.

balance. Turn your left foot out ever so slightly toward the target, maybe 10 degrees. If the left foot is set square, or perpendicular to the target line, you'll have to slide your hips toward the target on the downswing and hook the ball. If you set your left foot too far open—more than the 10 degrees I recommend, you'll tend to clear your hips early and quickly on the downswing, which promotes a fade.

Your right foot should be fanned out to the right about 10 degrees in relation to the target line so it mirrors the position of your left foot. If you turn the right foot in, it will restrict your turn. Fan the right foot too far out, and you'll promote a hook.

The right foot position isn't etched in stone, though. When I need an extra 10 yards out of a drive, I'll angle my right foot out a few degrees more than normal. That tends to increase the size of my turn and the length of my backswing. Any more than that, though, and I've reached a point of diminishing returns.

There's also the matter of weight distribution. I like it 50-50 on each foot. As for heel-to-toe weight distribution, I believe the weight should be right in the arch of each foot. I don't subscribe to the idea of placing your weight on the balls of your feet. That's too far forward and makes it difficult to push off your right foot at the beginning of the downswing. If your weight is back on your heels, you'll have extremely poor balance.

4. THE IMPORTANCE OF PERFECT POSTURE

Good posture at address sets the stage for a full, free body turn and arm swing. When you assume a sound upper body position at address, you should feel comfortable and balanced with no strain on your back. It should feel as natural as standing.

The most important part of good posture is bending properly from the hips at address (2-7). You don't want your upper body to droop lazily over the ball. You don't want to sag from the waist (2-8). By bending properly at the hips, you establish a feeling of straightness in your back. Your back isn't straight, of course, but it should feel that way.

2-7, 2-8: Bending properly at the hips (left) encourages full, correct turning with your upper body. Stooping over at the waist makes it impossible to perform an efficient backswing turn.

How far forward should you bend? Try this test: Lean forward from the hips, keeping your arms completely limp. Your arms should hang just over the front of your feet. This position gives your arms plenty of room to swing with no interference from your body. The forward bending of your torso also promotes an unrestricted turn with your upper body.

Another test: When you grip the club at address, the angle between your left forearm and the shaft should be obtuse or more than 90 degrees (2-9). If the left arm and clubshaft describe a straight line, you're either standing too far from the ball, or your posture is too upright. Your arms will be stiff and extended, which in turn increases your grip pressure—another no-no.

Practice bending from the hips frequently. You don't need a club

2-9: A good posture check is to review the relationship between the clubshaft and your left arm at address. They should form a slight angle. You don't want them to describe a straight, unbroken line.

to rehearse. Ingrain the sensation. Your posture, like your grip, should never vary from club to club. It's one of the game's constants and should become second nature.

YOUR BASIC, ALL-PURPOSE GOLF SWING

The most unusual shot for me is the simple, straightforward shot where I don't want the ball to fade or draw, or fly particularly high or low. For reasons I'll explain later, I like to curve the ball in one direction or another on almost every shot I play. Ever heard the saying, "The hardest shot in golf is the dead-straight shot?" Well, it's true. I can adjust my setup so the ball is guaranteed to fade or draw. But the hardest shot to bring off is the one that doesn't curve at all.

Nevertheless, that is the type of shot I'll describe here. All specialty shots—those that require *shotmaking*—are simply variations from the straight, no-frills shot I'm describing here. If I want to draw or fade the ball, I simply shift that alignment one direction or the other, make a couple of other adjustments and go. But all shotmaking starts with variations from a basic swing structured around the fundamentals I described earlier.

At address, my feet and shoulders are aligned slightly to the left of the target (*2-10*). The target line is established by a line running from the ball to the target, and my stance is defined by a line running parallel to the target line, much like railroad tracks.

2-10: For a straight shot, your feet, hips and upper body should be aligned almost parallel to the target line, much like railroad tracks.

2-11: At the beginning of the backswing, the turning of your shoulders should enact a shifting of weight onto your right foot.

THE FIRST PART OF THE BACKSWING

I initiate the backswing by turning my right hip and shoulder away from the ball. It's primarily a rotary action, but at the same time there is a shifting of the weight onto the right foot *(2-11)*. I don't believe in sliding the body to the right, though. The weight shift is taken care of simply by turning. Sliding laterally means wasted movement.

That first move back is critical and is done entirely by the body. Some instructors advocate swinging the club back with your arms and letting the body follow, but I disagree. It's too easy to swing your arms back on a different path every time. By simply turning the body and letting your hands and arms go along for the ride, you take the club back on the same path and plane every time. A good thought is to maintain the space between your left arm and torso until the shaft of the club is parallel to the ground.

Another key is to feel like your left shoulder is higher than the

2-12: During the first stage of the backswing, you should feel like your left shoulder is higher than your right. That isn't the case, as the photograph shows. But having that sensation will encourage a level, on-plane shoulder turn.

right at all times (*2-12*). If your left shoulder dips downward, you're not turning the shoulders, but merely tilting them. It makes for a very upright swing plane and poor weight shift.

When your hands reach waist-height, your wrists should begin to hinge and cock. This is a natural reaction; it should not be forced. In fact, don't worry about it. If your grip pressure is light and uniform, and your grip is sound, it will happen automatically.

AT THE TOP

At the top of the backswing, my only thought is to set the clubshaft parallel to the ground. You can swing the club back farther than that, but if you do it should not be accomplished by overcocking the wrists or letting your weight drift to your left side. If the club goes past parallel, it should be done by increasing your shoulder turn while keeping your upper body to the right of the ball.

2-13: The mark of a full backswing is involvement with every part of your body. The feet, knees, hips, shoulders, arms and hands all play a part in setting the stage for a powerful, flowing downswing.

Other sensations signal when you've completed the backswing. In photo *2-13*, my hips have turned about as far as they can go, and there's a sense of tautness in my lower back. But if I feel my left heel coming off the ground, I know I've swung back too far. *Your* left heel can rise, as long as it doesn't fly off the ground so far that you overswing or have difficulty planting it back down in exactly the same place.

Then there is the matter of the "straight left arm." I've never paid any attention to how straight my left arm is. If it bends a bit at the elbow, fine. The energy you accumulate on the downswing will straighten the left arm through impact, so what's the difference? The right arm is more important. At all times it should remain close to your right side, near your ribs. If it strays, you know you're performing the backswing with your arms alone, and that isn't correct. At the top, I like to feel that the position of my right elbow is fixed and that I've turned "around" it on the backswing. At the top, the right elbow should be hidden when looking at your swing from a face-on angle. That proves you've turned your body fully.

THE FIRST MOVE DOWN

The way you initiate the downswing determines a good or bad shot. Everything can be textbook perfect to this point, but a poor move early in the downswing can wreck it all. You have to get the sequence of motion correct, or you'll never have a chance of delivering the clubhead into the ball cleanly and powerfully.

The first move down is with the left shoulder (2-14). It moves down and to the left. I do not subscribe to the philosophy of the down-swing occurring "from the ground up." I feel that if I swing down with

2-14: The downswing begins by turning your left shoulder down and to the left. This allows for the proper sequence of motion with your upper and lower body.

my shoulders, my hips will follow. However, if I begin the downswing by turning my hips or driving with my legs, the shoulders don't necessarily have to follow. If the shoulders go first, it's much easier for everything to unwind naturally. You'll hit the ball solidly with greater consistency, and there's no loss of power. I'll hammer away at this theme more later.

IMPACT: TURNING ON
THE POWER

Just before impact, I apply all the power I can into the shot. There are some shots I'll try to hit harder than others, but I definitely try to exert some effort just before the clubhead strikes the ball. I don't advocate swinging lazily through impact. You'll hit the ball solidly more often if you apply some force late in the downswing.

I like to feel that I'm hitting the ball with my right hip *(2-15)*. That

2-15: The clubface must be square at impact, but it's dangerous to try to square it up with your hands. As you rotate your right hip on the downswing, think of the clubface rotating to a square position along with it.

may sound ridiculous, but I have the definite sensation that, as my hips unwind, my right hip mimics the squaring action of the clubface. I don't try to control the clubface with my hands. It's very difficult to time things properly with the small, fast-twitch muscles in your hands. I think of my right hip. Not only does the rotary action with the hips help square the clubface, it encourages me to turn my hips very quickly through impact, which supplies power and gives my arms the room necessary to swing the clubhead down along the correct swing path.

How do I insure that my clubhead approaches the ball along the correct swing path? I want to check my swing path constantly because if it's excessively inside-to-outside, I'll block or hook the ball. Too much outside-to-inside causes a pull or slice. To monitor my swing path, I like to swing halfway down from the top and freeze. I then examine the clubshaft. I want the handle pointing precisely in the direction where I want the ball to travel when it explodes off the clubface. If I want to hit a draw, I obviously want the butt end of the clubshaft to point out to the right, as that signifies an inside-to-outside swing path in relation to the target line. When I'm trying to hit the ball dead straight, I want the clubshaft to point directly at the target rather than to the right or left of it.

FOLLOW-THROUGH:
MORE THAN ESTHETICS

It's true that the follow-through is ineffectual in that the ball is already gone and there's nothing you can do to alter its flight. But the follow-through is a valuable learning tool because it reflects what occurred earlier in your swing. Moreover, by trying to accomplish a certain "look" on your follow-through, you'll have to make the club perform in a certain way prior to impact.

My primary objective on all standard shots is to straighten my right arm just after impact (2-16). When the clubhead has traveled one foot after impact, my right arm is dead straight. It almost looks like I'm chasing the ball out to the target. By doing this, I keep the clubhead traveling along the target line longer, and it helps me keep my upper

2-16: By straightening your right arm through impact, you'll keep the clubhead traveling down the target line longer.

body down through impact rather than rising up. My head stays down, too, all because of my right arm straightening.

A FANTASTIC FINISH

Far into my follow-through, at a point where my hands reach head-height, I like to feel 90 percent of my weight on my left foot. This demonstrates that I've shifted and turned through the ball aggressively, that the momentum has carried my body well to the left.

To discern whether you've shifted your weight fully, swing to a full finish and freeze your position. Now lift your right foot off the ground.

2-17, 2-18: At the finish of a full swing, momentum should carry almost all of your weight onto your left side. To check if you've accomplished this, lift your right foot. You should be able to balance on your left foot alone.

You should be able to stand on your left leg alone without losing your balance (*2-17, 2-18*).

I also like to finish with my back straight or perpendicular to the horizon. Don't go for the "reverse C" look. If you do, there's a good chance you've hung back on your right side through impact, and that runs contrary to your goal of imparting all of your weight and strength into hitting the ball. Your upper body should face the target.

The lessons that follow are structured to progress through all the clubs in your bag. As we move along, you'll find that I reiterate many of the principles involved in making a standard swing.

But that's all shotmaking is—making a standard swing with a few adjustments. That's the beauty of it. The golf swing isn't as complicated as it's been made out to be, and in no time at all you'll be hitting shots you never dreamed were possible.

Chapter 3

A 'WORKING' TEE SHOT

IN MANY WAYS THE DRIVE IS THE MOST IMPORTANT SHOT in the game. A good drive doesn't necessarily guarantee a par or birdie, but a poor drive can insure a bogey or worse. Excellent drivers of the ball usually have good control with the rest of their clubs, too. Because the swing with the driver is longer than with the other clubs, the shorter, more controlled swings with the irons are a piece of cake. Moreover, all the principles of good driving—fading and drawing the ball at will, playing high and low shots—apply to other shots, too. Master them with the driver, and there's a good chance you'll master them all.

From a shotmaking standpoint, the ability to work the ball off the tee can help you pull off what otherwise would be considered a low-percentage shot. At the 1987 Bob Hope Chrysler Classic, I came to the last hole tied with Bernhard Langer. In those days the tournament was played at the PGA West Stadium Course. The 18th hole there is a long par 4 that doglegs to the left. Water runs all along the left side of the hole. It's an extremely dangerous driving hole, particularly when you have to make a par. Hit it left, and you're wet. Bail out to the right, and you're left with an extremely long second shot to an elusive green.

To "fit" my tee shot to the hole, I would have to play a right-to-left draw. It was a sticky problem at that stage of my career. I felt uncomfortable trying to draw the ball. I just wasn't as versatile with my driver as some guys. I was really feeling the heat and wanted to go with my favorite tee shot, a slight fade. That meant I would have to start the ball out over the water and curve it to the right. If the ball failed to curve, a bogey or worse was almost certain.

I aligned my feet and shoulders toward a spot 10 yards into the water. I opened the clubface so it was square to a line bisecting the center of the fairway. Only then did I take my grip; I didn't want to grip the club and *then* twist the clubface open. I knew I had to swing the clubhead through the ball on a line running parallel with my feet. As long as the clubface remained open through impact, the ball would have to fade. I knew that is what would happen. I have a weak left-hand grip to begin with, so the chances of my rotating the clubface closed were small. I felt there was no way I could pull the ball to the left.

I made a smooth, silky swing, thinking only of maintaining my tempo. The ball started at the right edge of the water and curved gently to the right, finishing on the right side of the fairway. Bernhard followed with a perfect 3-wood shot that finished in the middle of the fairway. I then hit a 4-iron to the green that stopped 18 feet from the hole. Bernhard's approach shot finished farther from the hole than mine. He putted first and missed. Now it was my turn, and when I made the putt I jumped for joy. I had won, and that birdie on the last hole was set up through trust in my driver.

THE MYTH OF THE
STRING-STRAIGHT DRIVE

Some amateurs spend their whole golfing lives trying to hit the ball straight. I've always considered the straight ball the hardest shot to hit in golf and one of the most foolish to try to master. The conditions at impact have to be perfect (clubface square, clubhead traveling directly down the target line) to hit a shot with no curvature at all. In my life, I've only met one golfer who tried to hit a straight ball: Byron Nelson, who also was one of the most accurate drivers who ever lived. Byron told me that when he missed a shot with the driver, it was either a slight push or pull. Very seldom did he hook or slice. You can live with a push or a pull, but if you combine it with a hook or slice, you can really hit the ball wildly.

I know one thing: There is only one Byron Nelson.

The straight shot is difficult for other reasons. Say you're aiming for the center of the fairway. Now, if you hook or slice the ball, you in effect are cutting down your margin for error by one half. If you slice by accident, you only have half the width of the fairway to accommodate the miss. Any more, and you're in trouble.

On the other hand, what if you deliberately play a fade, but aim at the left edge of the fairway? If you hit a straight ball, your second shot is very playable. If you fade the ball the amount you intend, you're in perfect position. If you fade the ball too much, you have the entire width of the fairway as your landing area, plenty of room for even wild hitters. In effect, you're eliminating all the trouble to the left, while increasing your margin for error to the right.

I believe in working the ball on approach shots into the greens, too. But it's especially important with the driver. Always try to work the ball off the tee, if only by a few yards.

THE MOST IMPORTANT CONSIDERATION

The fundamentals never change, so even with the driver you should never tamper with your grip, stance width, knee flex or posture. But you *do* make one important adjustment at address to accommodate the different swing motion of the driver.

The essential difference between the driver and other clubs is that the clubhead of the driver is traveling slightly upward when it strikes the ball. Because the driver has so little loft, you need help getting the ball airborne. The "hit down, ball goes up" adage doesn't apply very well with the driver. You need to adjust your setup so you're catching the ball on the upswing. This is true on all standard shots with the driver.

3-1: By positioning the ball just inside your left heel, you'll deliver a slightly ascending blow and insure getting the ball airborne.

The chief consideration is ball position. With the driver you want to place the ball well forward in your stance, just inside your left heel (*3-1*). That's the standard ball-position "rule" for many players, and it works for me. Because the lowest point in your swing arc is on a line directly below your chin, positioning the ball forward of that point will insure that the clubhead is traveling upward at impact. Note that because my stance is fairly wide, playing the ball off my left heel effectively moves it farther forward than for most players. If you choose a narrower stance (which I don't recommend), it will affect your ball position. If you addressed the ball with your feet close together and played the ball off your left heel, it would be too far back in your stance. So make sure your stance width is consistent.

BASIC WEAPONRY:
DRAWING AND FADING

Every golfer has a natural shot shape. Your natural, no-frills swing will produce either a fade or a draw most of the time. For 90 percent of amateurs, that shot is a fade—or a slice, as the case may be. There is nothing wrong with a fade, but when the tee shot calls for a draw, real trouble sets in. Making the type of swing necessary to produce a draw forces the slicer to make a swing that mechanically is opposite of the swing they're accustomed to making. It's a sickening, helpless feeling, and I identify and sympathize with it. My natural shot is a fade, and early in my career I wanted to hit the fade whenever possible. I could hit a draw, of course. But my margin for error was smaller and the outcome wasn't always predictable. I might push the ball or hit a pull-hook. I wasn't consistent.

As I struggled to build a swing that would produce a dependable, controlled draw, I learned something very important: *You can curve the ball either way without changing your swing.* The natural swing that produces a fade can also produce a draw, providing you make a couple of refinements in your setup and clubface position at address. You do need to formulate a swing that is basically sound, one that adheres to the principles I outlined in Chapter 2. But once you establish a correct, basic swing, drawing and fading the ball at will isn't difficult at all.

It helps to understand what makes the ball draw to begin with. Physics demands that the clubhead be traveling on an inside-to-outside path in relation to the target line. The clubface must be closed or aiming to the left of the target line at the moment of impact. That's what imparts the counterclockwise sidespin that causes the ball to curve from right to left.

What most slicers do in their effort to draw the ball is exaggerate that inside-to-outside swing motion. It doesn't work. The torso doesn't turn enough or turns too much in relation to the swinging of the hands and arms. The body gets all tangled up, disrupting tempo and timing. Worse yet, they get a false sense of feedback as to what the clubhead actually is doing through impact. The player may *feel* that the clubhead is swinging from the inside, when in fact it may still be swinging from outside-to-inside. You may work at trying to draw the ball, but the methodology is so flawed, the procedure so fundamentally wrong, that you never develop a draw you can count on. It's why golfers who slice try for years to solve the problem and never do.

I've found that if you adjust your alignment, you can rearrange your swing path naturally and forget about trying to swing differently. Learning to draw or fade the ball becomes very simple. And the method I use not only works for the driver, it works for every club in the bag.

HOW TO
DRAW THE BALL

The draw, which curves from right to left for a right-handed player, has several advantages. It's great when you need maximum distance because the ball tends to penetrate the air like a bullet. It flies a little lower than a fade due to the clubface being closed slightly at address. Thus, it is the most effective distance shot when you're playing into a headwind. It also is useful when the fairways are firm. A draw strikes the ground on a flatter, shallower angle, providing maximum roll and extra yards. What's more, the draw has less backspin on it than a fade due to the closed clubface and the shallower angle of attack with the clubhead. That helps it roll farther, too.

To draw the ball, you need only make two adjustments. The first is with your alignment. At address, set your feet and upper body so they're aimed to the right of your target (3-2). By aiming to the right, my normal swing will deliver the clubhead into the ball on a path that's inside-to-outside in relation to the target line.

Second, I aim the clubface at the target, the spot where I want the ball to end up. The clubface, then, is square to the target but aimed well to the left of where my feet and upper body are aligned.

Now I just make my normal swing. The ball will start out where my feet and shoulders are aligned, but because my clubface is closed, the ball will acquire counterclockwise sidespin and curve back to the left. The amount I want to draw the ball is determined by how drastically I align my body to the right of the target at address.

3-2: Recipe for a right-to-left draw: My feet and hips are aligned to the right on the line where I want the ball to begin its flight. The clubface is aimed at the center of the fairway, where I want the ball to land.

If this prescription doesn't produce immediate results, try adding the following swing keys. First, when you swing the clubhead through the ball, think of straightening your right arm. This will help you fully release the clubhead through impact, returning it to the position you established at address. Your right arm should straighten and extend *down the line you want the ball to start.* You don't want to swing your arms toward the target, the spot where you want the ball to come to rest. That would mean you're swinging outside-to-inside relative to your body lines, the very thing that causes a slice.

HOW TO
FADE THE BALL

The fade isn't complicated at all because essentially it's played in just the opposite manner of the draw. For most golfers the fade is the easier shot to play, as they find it easier to swing the club from outside-to-inside rather than inside-to-outside.

The fade is predicated on control more than distance. The standard left-to-right shot generally flies higher than a draw due to the clubface being open at impact. (An open clubface serves to increase loft on the clubface.) The increased loft of the clubface means a higher backspin rate, which makes it climb higher and stay airborne longer.

Because a fade flies higher, it's more at the mercy of the wind. At the same time, the fade possesses less sidespin than a draw and thus will curve less. Ever hear of a "duck hook," the shot that dives sharply to the left just after impact? Well, there is no such thing as a "duck slice" because the fade simply doesn't have as much sidespin. That's why it's a control shot. Regardless of how much you fade the ball, if you aim far enough to the left, it's hard to miss the shot to the right. Furthermore, because the fade flies higher, it strikes the ground at an angle more toward the vertical, which means it runs less after landing.

3-3: The formula for a fade is the just the opposite as for a draw. I align my feet and shoulders to the left of the target, while aiming the clubface where I want the ball to land.

It's no accident that some of the best drivers in the game have used the fade as their bread-and-butter shot. Sam Snead, Ben Hogan, Jack Nicklaus and Lee Trevino, just to name a few, are among the most accurate drivers in history, and all are notorious for fading the ball when they *had* to hit the fairway.

To fade the ball, I set up with my feet and shoulders aligned to the left of the target (3-3). The clubface is set open in relation to my body lines but is square to the target. Your gripping procedure is critical, and to better see how the clubface is affected, I've chosen a 5-iron *(below)*. The set-up procedure is the same for the driver. I make sure that I open the clubface first (3-4), then complete my grip (3-5). Many amateurs take their normal grip and then twist the clubface open. That isn't an

3-4, 3-5: *A crucial step in fading the ball is to establish the clubface position first (left). Only after you aim the clubface should you complete your grip.*

open clubface at all. At impact you'll return the clubface to a square position and hit a pull instead of a fade.

When I've finished with my preshot adjustments, I then make my normal swing, thinking only of swinging the club through the ball along the line established by my feet and shoulders.

That sounds almost too simple, but it's the most effective method I know. You want to avoid getting too fancy. Never try to manipulate the clubface with your hands through impact. Timing the release perfectly is just too difficult. Nor should you consciously try to maintain the open clubface position by curbing clubface rotation through impact. I also advise against tinkering with your ball position, unless you're trying to adjust the height of the shot. Some players, you know, find it easier to fade the ball by placing it farther forward in their stance. Or they tinker with their grip, making it "weaker" so the clubface can't rotate closed. All of these adjustments are unnecessary and only add variables to the equation. Keep it simple and work hard to perfect it.

EFFECTIVE
TEEING TACTICS

In golf you should always think one shot ahead, and that strategy begins before you strike the first shot. The tee is the only place where you have the ball in hand and can decide for yourself where you want to play the shot from. It's an underrated part of the game. By teeing the ball on the side of the teeing ground that best suits the type of shot you are playing, you effectively widen the fairway and improve the position of the ball for your second shot.

The basic rule is this: If you want to fade the ball, tee up on the right side of the teeing ground. If you're playing a draw, tee up on the left. That alone will increase the area of the landing zone. To make the fairway play even wider, adjust your aim. If you tee up on the right side of the tee to accommodate a left-to-right fade, aim for the left side of the fairway.

When I'm playing a draw, I sometimes tee the ball on the extreme left-hand side of the teeing ground with my ball placed just inside the tee marker. I actually stand outside of the teeing ground, which is permitted by the Rules of Golf.

Alignment is extremely important on your tee shot. A common mistake is to align yourself in the direction the teeing ground runs. This falls right into the hands of the course architect, who may deviously have constructed the teeing ground so it points left or right of the fairway. When the superintendent mows the teeing ground, the mowing strips run parallel to the teeing ground, which also could sucker you into aligning yourself too far left or right. It's a subtle trick. Just remember to align your feet and shoulders to a distant point in the fairway. Pay no attention to local features.

HOW HIGH SHOULD
YOU TEE THE BALL?

This is another critical area that many amateurs don't pay much attention to. Most of my pro-am partners tee the ball any old way, devoting about two seconds to the whole procedure. They seem to have a "favorite" height they use on every tee shot, regardless of the type of shot they are going to play. They put themselves at a huge disadvantage right there. The height you tee the ball affects the trajectory of the shot

3-6: For a standard trajectory, tee the ball so the top of the clubhead matches up with the ball's equator.

and also facilitates fading or drawing. The standard teeing height is the ball's equator matching up with the top of the clubhead (3-6).

Here is the formula for hitting high and low shots:

For a low shot, tee the ball lower. There are three occasions when I like to hit the ball low. First, I like a low shot when the wind is howling in my face or from the side. A low shot performs much better in a headwind or crosswinds from either direction because the ball doesn't spin as much. A low shot is much like a baseball pitcher's knuckleball and tends to penetrate through the wind. Also, wind speeds are lower near the ground than at higher elevations, so it makes sense to keep the ball "under" the fiercest part of wind. Second, I prefer a low shot when the ground is firm and allows plenty of roll. It's a great way to obtain extra distance. Third, you will always hit the ball straighter when you tee it low. The ball simply doesn't hang in the air as long and thus has less time to careen into trouble.

With the driver, trajectory is determined by the height you tee the ball. With irons and fairway woods, trajectory is determined by ball position—the farther back you play the ball, the lower the ball flies. But it's no good playing the ball farther back in your stance with the driver because that decreases the loft of the clubface too much. You turn a 10-degree driver into a 7-degree driver, and that isn't enough to hit the ball

3-7: To hit the ball low, address the ball so the center of the clubface matches up with a point just below the ball's equator.

sufficiently high in the air. Moreover, when you play the ball back, you promote a downward blow, and again there's not enough loft on the driver to get the ball airborne.

To obtain a low, boring trajectory, I tee the ball low, so the center of the clubface matches up with a point just below the ball's equator (3-7). You never want to tee the ball lower than that because you can't make solid contact. When you tee the ball low, you are forced to swing the clubhead through the ball at a very shallow angle, the clubhead traveling almost level with the ground at impact. Because you aren't delivering a steep, upward blow, you are relying more on the loft of the clubface to get the ball in the air.

For a high shot, tee the ball higher. I go with a high shot when I'm playing downwind or when I need to carry an obstacle such as a bunker, creek or the corner of a dogleg. I also will go with a higher shot when the ground is soggy because I have to compensate for the lack of roll. For maximum carry, I tee the ball so the majority of the ball rests higher than the top of the clubhead (3-8). Again, I take special care not to move the ball back in my stance. If anything, I'll nudge it forward an inch. This not only encourages an upward blow with the clubhead, it effectively increases the loft of the clubface. I've turned a 10-degree driver into a 12-degree driver.

3-8: For a high shot and extra carry, tee the ball so most of the ball is above the top of the clubhead.

A word of caution about playing the ball farther forward than usual. The farther forward you position the ball, the more you'll tend to swipe across the ball from outside-to-inside, which promotes a pull to the left or a slice. You can only swing the clubhead down the target line so far before it wants to swing to the left. So, you have to make a special effort to "stay with the shot." You have to keep your head well back or behind the ball through impact. Your head and upper body must stay down as well. The thought that helps me achieve this is to extend my right arm down the target line after impact, letting it straighten at the elbow. This keeps the clubhead moving aggressively and will prevent the clubface from closing.

One other thing to remember: Regardless of the height you tee the ball, you're swinging at the ball without respect to where it sits in relation to the ground. That may sound odd, but when some amateurs tee the ball low, they subconsciously fear striking the ground behind the ball. The thought of hitting a driver shot "fat" causes them to hit down on the ball. A similar phenomenon happens when they tee the ball high. The ball sits so high off the ground, they feel they have to swing up on the ball excessively to hit it solidly. They raise their head and spine. Practice getting your posture and ball position correct at address, then make your normal swing. Think of swinging at the ball, not the ground.

THE SEARCH FOR
THE PERFECT DRIVER

Next to the putter and the sand wedge, the driver is the most "individual" club in the bag. Many golfers spend years searching for the perfect driver, and when they find one they like, they'll stay with it for as long as it lasts. It's a highly personal club. In my case, I used the same persimmon driver for years and trusted it implicitly. I knew its idiosyncrasies, what I had to do to work the ball the way I wanted. It was like an old friend. A couple of years ago, I finally found a metal-headed driver I liked, and after months of reluctant experimentation, convinced myself it was better. That experience underscored how indispensable a good driver can be. If you're running around in circles trying to find the perfect driver, here are a couple of tips that will expedite your search.

Let your home course determine driver loft.

Some golfers naturally hit the ball low, others high. The same 10-degree driver behaves quite differently in the hands of different players. So for me to prescribe a specific loft without watching you play would be silly. However, if you evaluate the conditions of your home course, its features and design, the answer will come into focus. Here are the rules:

Go with less loft if:
- The fairways are firm and hard
- The wind blows most of the time
- Your course is at sea level
- The air is usually damp and heavy
- You are a wild hitter

Go with more loft if:
- The course is wide-open with few hazards
- You are a straight hitter
- You are good enough to hit the driver off the fairway
- There is a preponderance of dogleg holes
- You are a short hitter
- The fairways are soft
- You play at high altitudes

Shaft flex: Try, try again.

It's harder than ever to make sense of shaft flex. There is a huge number of shafts on the market made of all types of materials, including steel, titanium, graphite and aluminum. Every manufacturer has a different idea of what "stiff" or "medium" means and classifies those flexes within a range they created. Unfortunately, there is no industry standard, so the stiff shaft made by one manufacturer might be another company's medium.

Adding to the confusion is the way each player swings. Two golfers can have identical swing speeds at impact, but that doesn't necessarily mean they need the same shaft flexes. If one golfer accelerates the club gradually on the downswing, the flexing characteristics of his shaft will differ from the golfer who accelerates the club suddenly and abruptly.

The considerations go well beyond simple shaft flex, too. There is torque, the amount the shaft twists during the swing. Torque helps determine whether the clubface is square or open at impact. There is "flex point," the location on the shaft where most of the bending occurs. The flex point has some effect on the launch angle of the ball at impact.

With all of this, the only way to find the right shaft for you is to experiment. Go to the range with two drivers that are identical except for shaft flex. One should be stiff, the other medium. Hit 20 balls with each one, alternating drivers every five shots or so. Pay attention to the following factors:

- *Feedback.* What kind of feel was translated through your arms and hands at impact? Generally, graphite shafts offer a softer, more fluid feel. Steel, on the other hand, may convey a more vivid feeling of impact. Are you able to discern which way the ball flew without looking up right after impact?
- *Which direction does the ball fly?* If you are missing shots to the right and you get a "clunky" sensation at impact, the shaft is most likely too stiff.
- *Note the range of your misses.* It may be that the "medium" or "regular" shaft flexes feel softer and provide a very nice sense of feedback. But does the ball fly in all directions? If that's the case, lean toward a stiffer shaft. Generally speaking, a softer, "whippier" shaft is more difficult to control, especially if you're a fairly long hitter.

I realize this is a chapter about driving, but this test applies to the irons as well. Find out which shaft flex is best before you buy. Switching shafts after you've bought the set can be frustrating—and expensive.

THREE NEAT SHOTS

No. 1: How to get 15 more yards

One of the big differences between a top pro and rank amateur is that the pro has extra power in reserve when he needs it. The amateur tends to go all-out on every drive, while the professional tends to hold back a bit until he comes to the long, wide-open par 4 or the par 5 he wants to reach in two. Then, making what appears to be the same smooth swing, *boom!* The ball suddenly goes 10 to 30 yards farther. What isn't apparent to the amateur is that the pro does this not through a more ferocious effort but by technical adjustments made at address and during the swing.

The situation: You've come to a medium-length par 5 with a wide fairway and no trouble in the landing area except for a fairway bunker on the left. Water fronts the green; an average-length drive will leave you a considerable distance from the front of the green, too far to risk

3-9: *The first step for getting extra yards is to set up for a draw. Align your body to the right, aim the clubface at the target and play the ball forward in your stance.*

49

trying to get home with a big 3-wood shot. But a big drive, one 15 yards farther than standard, will leave you within striking distance of the green with the 3-wood. If you get home in two, a birdie is very likely and an eagle is an outside possibility.

The setup: For maximum distance, you want to hit a high draw off the tee—the draw to provide maximum distance by getting extra roll, height to give you plenty of carry as well. To program the draw, align your feet and shoulders to the right-center of the fairway, the clubface square to the center of the fairway (3-9). To insure height on the shot, position the ball an extra inch forward in your stance, so you can hit up on the ball and counter the loss of clubface loft that results from closing the clubface at address. Finally, you need a slightly longer backswing to give the clubhead more time to accumulate speed on the downswing. So turn your right foot out an extra inch to the right, which will allow you to turn your shoulders farther without straining.

The swing: Timing is everything. Because you're making a longer

3-10: A bigger turn means a longer swing and more clubhead speed. For more distance, increase your shoulder turn so the club travels beyond parallel— or at least as far as you can comfortably swing it.

backswing, you need to maintain your balance at all times. The key is to be very deliberate on the backswing, so everything falls into place easily and in the proper sequence. Swing the club back slowly, feeling your weight shift to the right. At the top, think of the position of the club—it should be farther past parallel than usual *(3-10)*, which is fine. Start the downswing slowly. Don't "jump" on the shot. Let everything—shoulders, hips, feet, arms and hands—fire naturally.

Late in the downswing, think only of hitting the ball hard. I don't think "fast" because that connotes a loss of control. You want to swing as aggressively as you can through impact. As you do that, extend your right arm toward the spot where you aligned your body—the right-center of the fairway.

No. 2: Low screamer from the fairway

Some players reject the idea of using the driver anywhere except off the tee. It's not a bad rule of thumb—a fairway wood is fail-safe in

3-11: To hit the driver from the fairway, you need a steeper angle of approach and more loft than the driver provides. The key to getting both is to set up open.

most circumstances. But if your lie in the fairway is good, the ball perched up so you can deliver a precise, level blow, the driver is a good choice. You'll get a lot of roll because the ball flies lower, and if the wind is blowing against you, you'll actually get more distance than with a fairway wood.

The situation: You're playing a par 5 and have hit a mediocre drive into the fairway. The ground is firm and the ball is sitting up nicely. A solid hit will put you within chipping distance of the green, and even a mis-hit will give you little more than a wedge to the hole. You've been hitting your driver well all day.

The setup: The key is to set up as though you are playing a fade. Align your feet well to the left of the target line and set the clubface open in relation to your stance line *(3-11)*. The open clubface increases the loft of the clubface, which will help you get the ball airborne. What's more, by setting up open you're promoting a steeper angle of approach with the driver, the clubhead approaching the ball from the outside. That reduces the chance of a fat shot or the dreaded "drop kick." The driver will send the ball out lower, so the ball won't have enough "hang time" to soar into trouble.

3-12—3-14: To reach a long par 3 with your driver, you need to make the ball land softly. Begin by setting up open, your feet and shoulders aligned well to the left of your target, the clubface aimed at the green. Next, swing the club back along your body lines so the shaft of the club is parallel with your feet at the top of the swing. Through impact, swing the club directly along the line established by your feet. The outside-to-inside swing in relation to the green will produce the high, soft fade you're looking for.

So, you've aligned your feet and body slightly to the left, while aiming the clubface where you want the ball to finish. You also should position the ball about two inches inside your left heel, which is extremely far back for the driver, but which is acceptable because you've increased the clubface loft and want to deliver a slightly downward blow.

The swing: Nothing fancy here. Everything was preprogrammed at address. Your only thought should be to "stay with" the shot through impact, trying to penetrate the ground at a point just ahead of the ball. Your open stance will prevent a long swing, but that's fine. Your goal is solid club-ball contact, and a shorter swing makes that part a lot easier.

No. 3: Bring the long par 3 within reach

Rarely will you see a par-3 hole that's too far to reach with a long iron or fairway wood. But it does happen, usually on those 220-yard brutes when the wind is in your face, it's cold or a protecting bunker prevents you from landing the ball short and running it up to the green. Few feelings in golf are as frustrating as when you aren't able to reach a green in regulation purely because you don't hit the ball far enough.

When you reach the outside limits of your 3-wood distance, the

natural progression is to go with the driver. But while the 3-wood may not be enough club, the driver may be too much if you play your standard shot. The difference in the maximum distances of those two clubs can be as much as 40 yards. What's more, the characteristics of the driver shot may not fit the long par 3. You need the ball to hold the green, and the standard drive flies too low and hard—if you don't know how to make it do otherwise.

The situation: You're playing with the "A" players at your club, and they're hitting from the back tees. You come to a par 3 measuring 215 yards, the outside distance of your 3-wood. Compounding the distance problem is the wind—in your face and slightly from the left. You reach for the driver.

The setup: You'll want to hit a slice here—not a fade but a slice because a fade flies farther than a slice. Align your feet and shoulders much farther to the left than normal, as much as 30 yards *(3-12)*. Grip the club an inch lower down the handle than normal to shorten your swing arc and, consequently, the distance you hit the ball. Aim the clubface at the center of the green. The open clubface effectively increases loft, which eliminates the possibility of a low, hot ball flight. Finally, tee the ball higher than normal, further insurance you'll hit the ball high so it lands softly upon hitting the green.

The swing: At the top, the clubshaft should be parallel with your stance line, pointing to the left of the target *(3-13)*. When you aim well left of the target, the tendency is to pull your right arm in close to your body just after impact in a subconscious effort to cut across the ball so it slices far enough to the right. This is called "cutting off the swing," and it isn't necessary. You don't need to help the ball slice because the slice is pre-programmed by your setup. When you cut off your swing, you'll slice the ball too much or deliver a glancing blow that doesn't reach the green.

Think only of swinging powerfully along your body lines *(3-14)*, extending your arm down the target line well after impact. The ball will curve a lot, but it will do so in a penetrating, decisive manner. It will carry the required distance and land softly enough to hold the green.

Chapter 4

SHAPING YOUR FAIRWAY WOODS

HAD ALMOST ANY OTHER PGA TOUR PLAYER been in my place on the final hole at Shinnecock Hills, it's fairly certain he wouldn't have left himself with a 4-wood shot to the final green. He would have boomed a much longer drive than I did and thus would have had considerably less than 228 yards to the hole for the second shot. Because almost every other pro is longer on the second shot than me as well, in the end he would have had a middle iron to that well-protected green.

Under the pressure of the moment, however, the consequences of crushing a long drive can be summarized in two words: "native fescue." The long hitters were more apt to hit the ball in trouble. So distance wasn't my concern. My goal was to put the ball in the fairway so I'd have a clear shot at the green and a reasonable chance of making a par. Was I worried about the large amount of real estate I had to cover with the 4-wood? Not really, because I know that fairway woods aren't just distance clubs. They are terrific scoring clubs, too.

All my life I've been a relatively short hitter, and there was a time when I believed I was at a serious disadvantage to bigger, stronger players. But as I became more proficient at hitting my fairway woods, I came to realize I wasn't as much at a disadvantage as I first thought. I found my ability with fairway woods actually worked in my favor because not only was I able to hit the greens with them, I became better than average at hitting them from the rough, laying up on par 5s and hitting them from poor lies in the fairway.

Like I said, fairway woods can be offensive weapons. In the third round of the 1986 Masters, I was within three shots of the lead coming to the 15th hole, a medium-length par 5 with a large pond fronting the green. I hit a good drive—for me—and was left with 215 yards to the hole. A slight breeze was blowing in my face, so a 2-iron was out of the question. My ball was on the upslope of one of those "chocolate drop" mounds in the fairway. The hole was on the front right of the green.

I chose a 4-wood. The shot required a high trajectory so the ball would land softly on the firm Augusta National green, and a slight draw. I programmed them in at address. I aimed my feet and shoulders to the right and aimed the clubface square to the hole. I didn't position the ball forward in my stance because the extra height I needed was supplied by my ball sitting on the upslope of the mound. Instead I positioned the ball just forward of center.

From there I made my normal swing, thinking only of tempo and rhythm so I wouldn't lose my balance. When the ball was in the air, I turned to my caddie and said, "That thing is perfect." It almost was. The ball landed just short of the pin and stopped one foot from the hole. The resulting eagle put me within one shot of the lead. I didn't win that year, as it turned out. Some guy named Nicklaus won.

EVERYMAN'S
UTILITY CLUBS

To me, real shotmaking begins with the fairway woods. You can hit them high and low with ease, fade or draw them, hit them from perfect lies or out of divots. You can vary the distance they fly by making very small adjustments. They are the most forgiving clubs on mis-hits, the easiest clubs to hit in the air. For most golfers, fairway woods are far easier to use than long irons, which demand strength and great skill to hit well consistently. They are simply more practical, and a look in any amateur's bag proves it: The long irons are usually shiny and new, the grips fresh and tacky, while the fairway woods show signs of use.

The secret to their versatility lies in their design. The clubheads have the vast majority of their weight in the sole. The lower the weight is distributed, the easier it is to get the ball airborne. On most fairway woods, there's also plenty of weight distributed along the perimeter of the clubhead, and that makes the clubs effective even on off-center hits. They're very forgiving.

Fairway woods are considerably shorter than the driver, another control factor. The shorter the club, the easier it is to control the club-face. Fairway woods also possess generous loft. A 4-wood has more loft (usually in the 15-degree range) than a low iron, making it easier to carry the ball longer distances. The added loft also means less sidespin, so you're less likely to slice or hook the ball into trouble.

FUNDAMENTAL CHANGES:
BALL POSITION, HANDS AT ADDRESS

The fact that fairway woods have more loft than the driver necessitates a fundamental change in your setup. On all standard fairway wood shots, you want to hit the ball with a very slight descending blow. You don't need to worry about driving the ball into the turf or hitting the ball too low because the clubface loft causes the ball to become airborne immediately after impact.

For a conventional shot from a good lie in the fairway, position the ball forward of center in your stance, but a good two inches to the right of where you place the ball for the driver (4-1). When you deliver the slight downward blow, the ball will come out low and hard, but with sufficient height to provide maximum carry.

Your stance and posture never change, as I explained earlier. One factor to be aware of is the position of your hands relative to the ball at address. You don't want to shove your hands forward in order to "help" you hit down on the ball. Nor should your hands be placed behind the ball in an effort to help it into the air. If your hands were well behind

4-1: Because the ball position for the fairway wood shot is slightly more toward the center of your stance, you'll deliver a downward blow and utilize the loft of the clubface.

4-2: To promote the necessary downward blow through impact, position your hands slightly ahead of the ball at address.

the ball at address, for example, at impact they'll be farther forward than that position and the clubface will be open. That means a slice. Your hands should be just to the left of center of your body (4-2) with the clubface aiming down the intended line of flight. The idea is to position your hands at the place where they'll be at impact.

With my ball position taken care of and my hands stationed properly at address, I just make my normal swing. I obtain a normal ball flight, too—hard, accurate and solid. But there are two specialty shots you can use often that require creativity and definitely fall into the shot-making category.

TECHNIQUE NO. 1:
THE SWEEP

Occasionally you'll encounter a situation where the fairway is open and the area near the green is free of hazards. Your primary goal is pure dis-

4-3: Begin the "sweep" with the fairway wood by taking the club back low.

tance, although you want to maintain a reasonable degree of accuracy. You want maximum carry and a good bit of roll, too. It's a situation that calls for a sweeping-type blow through impact because there's no better way to get distance.

To sweep the ball cleanly, position the ball forward in your stance, about where you would for a drive. Your lie must be good with the ball sitting up nicely on the turf. As you start the backswing, keep the club low to the ground *(4-3)* because you'll want it to approach the ball in the same level fashion. Make a longer backswing than normal *(4-4)*, taking care not to let your head drift to the right. At the top, go ahead and let the clubshaft extend a bit past parallel. On the downswing, keep your head centered and straighten your right arm through impact.

4-4: Because the pur-pose of the "sweep" is to get extra yards, make a bigger turn than normal and allow the club to travel past parallel.

4-5: Because the "sweep" doesn't require downward penetration with the club-head through impact, allow your head to come up after the ball is gone.

Think only of brushing the grass directly below the ball. You don't want to bang down on the ball.

Because the ball is positioned forward, the clubhead will be traveling level with the turf at impact. The ball will explode off the clubface with minimal backspin and stay airborne a long time. The lack of backspin will also cause the ball to roll a great deal after landing.

One other key: After impact, let your head come up along with the clubhead (4-5). Although the ball is long gone, you're still promoting a level angle of approach prior to impact.

Swinging all-out can be risky on other shots, but I seldom worry about going astray with this shot. If you hit the ball thin, you'll lose a bit of distance but the ball will still travel pretty far. Don't worry about hitting the shot fat, even though your ball is positioned forward—keeping your head still throughout the swing will prevent that.

TECHNIQUE NO. 2:
THE PINCH

You're playing the same par-5 hole, only this time you've hit a longer drive and can reach the green with ease. The problem is, the green is very firm and you need to land the ball softly to make it hold. In this case, you need plenty of backspin and a fairly high ball flight. Consider trying the "pinch," a swing in which the clubhead penetrates the ground *after* impact.

The first consideration with the pinch is to move the ball back in your stance, about six inches inside your left heel (appreciably farther back than for a standard fairway wood shot). Second, make your backswing a little steeper, the clubhead rising abruptly early in the backswing and moving almost vertically when your hands reach hip height. Your top-of-backswing position should be more upright than normal *(4-6)* due to

4-6: *A steep backswing means a steep angle of descent on the downswing. With the "pinch" shot, you want to hit down sharply on the back of the ball.*

the steeper takeaway and your desire to hit down sharply on the ball. Because this shot is designed more for accuracy than distance, don't turn your body excessively or let the club swing back too far.

On the downswing, think of delivering the clubhead into the ball on the same steep angle you took it back on. Hit down sharply into the back of the ball and try to take a divot about one inch in front of the ball. Keep your head down well after impact; this insures that your upper body stays down as well, a key to delivering a downward blow.

The pinch is not a "knockdown" shot. Don't make any adjustments in your swing to deloft the clubface and hit the ball low. You want a trajectory that is sufficiently high to allow the ball to hit the green on a steep angle. That, combined with the backspin achieved by hitting down on the ball, will allow you to hold the green for an easy two-putt birdie.

HITTING FROM ROUGH

The real value of fairway woods is their effectiveness from rough. At the 1995 Nissan Open, my drive on the par-4 12th hole landed in deep rough and set up a very worrisome second shot over a deep barranca. I had to carry the ball only 140 yards to clear the barranca, but my lie was so horrible I wasn't sure I could get across with any iron shot. The fact that I had 165 yards to the hole seemed almost incidental.

I studied the shot for quite a while before electing to use my 4-wood. I choked down on the handle and opened my stance considerably, which also served to open the clubface. I chopped down viciously on the ball and hoped for the best. The result was startling. The ball cleared the barranca and bounded forward just left of the green. From there I had an easy chip and a one-putt par, and I went on to win the tournament handily.

Under normal circumstances there is nothing heroic about a 165-yard shot with a 4-wood, but it was the only way I could get the ball close to the green in two. And it illustrates how versatile fairway woods really are. From the rough they're superb. The rounded structure of the clubhead tends to glide through tall grass, whereas the sharp leading edge of an iron tends to snag and turn the clubface closed, leading to a smothered shot. Fairway woods also have greater mass along the sole, which helps get the ball up in the air. Finally, fairway woods are simply bulkier than irons and plow through the rough better.

KNOW YOUR
LIMITATIONS

The first rule when your ball is in rough is not to exceed your capabilities. Fairway woods almost always are more effective than long irons, but there comes a point where even fairway woods won't advance the ball to the extent you desire. Experience will teach you when to give up on the idea of trying to hit a heroic fairway wood and merely try to get the ball back onto the fairway.

4-7—4-9: From rough, play the ball back in your stance to encourage a downward blow through impact. On the backswing, keep a good portion of your weight on your left side to promote an upright backswing and cleaner club-ball contact. Remember to make a full turn to generate plenty of clubhead speed.

A PLAY IN
THREE ACTS

The following three-step procedure will not only get you out of the rough, but advance the ball farther forward than you dreamed possible. First, *play the ball back in your stance* (4-7). If your lie is especially bad, try placing the ball to the right of center in your stance. Remember, this positioning will deloft the clubface so you'll need a fairway wood with extra loft in order to get the ball in the air. The ball-back directive assures that you'll hit down more steeply on the ball, which is smart because less grass will tend to interfere with the movement of the clubhead.

Second, *place at least 60 percent of your weight on your left foot at address and try to maintain that weight distribution throughout the swing.* Keeping your weight on your left side promotes a more upright backswing (4-8) and a downswing that delivers the clubhead into the ball on a steeper angle to avoid catching the grass behind the ball.

On the backswing, avoid the tendency of merely lifting your arms into position. Remember to turn your body *(4-9)*. It's a shot that requires some force.

Finally, *hit down sharply on the ball*. This is pretty much assured by your ball position and keeping your weight on your left side throughout the swing, but harboring that thought will help you accomplish it even more assertively. Through impact, think of hitting the ball, not the grass, and of letting the clubhead drive down and through the shot.

What type of ball flight can you expect? Generally, the longer and thicker the grass, the lower the ball will fly, the less spin it will have and the farther it will roll after landing. Don't be too ambitious about fading or drawing the ball. The grass acts as a lubricant and will prevent you from imparting enough sidespin to make the ball curve.

HITTING A 3-WOOD
FROM THE TEE

Returning to Riviera Country Club for a moment, the 10th hole is a very short par 4, so short that some of my fellow pros try to drive the green. I never hit a driver on that hole. If I did and missed the shot to the right, I would have no second shot at all. If I pulled the ball to the left, a fairway bunker awaits and I'd have a 50-yard sand shot, one of the most difficult in golf to play well. I opt for the 3-wood, both for the way it helps me keep the ball in play and because it leaves me with an optimum distance—80 yards or so—to play my second shot with a sand wedge. It's a good example of playing "aggressive defense" off the tee.

Most amateurs reach for the driver instinctively on every par 4 and par 5. In my opinion, they underrate their potential with the 3-wood. In fact, even though I'm a short hitter, I hit a 3-wood off the tee when I feel accuracy is more important than distance. Even without seeing you play, I can recommend you use the 3-wood off the tee more often.

Here are the situations where you should play the 3-wood off the tee:

• *If you're a short hitter and the fairways are lush.* Even a forceful low shot won't roll much when conditions are wet, and you want to carry the ball as far as possible.

- *When you're driving downwind.* Not many amateurs realize it, but wind has a way of knocking the ball out of the sky even when the wind is with you. If you use the driver downwind, the ball gets on the ground in a hurry. Consider the 3-wood, as the extra loft means a longer carry and, frequently, a longer tee shot than with the driver.
- *When playing a dogleg.* Nothing is more frustrating than hitting your ball through the fairway on a hole that curves sharply in the landing zone. The idea is to hit a high shot that stops quickly after it lands.
- *When you must keep the ball in play.* It's one thing to have a long second shot from the fairway, quite another to not have a second shot at all because your drive is in jail. Because the 3-wood has extra loft, you impart less sidespin and the ball is less likely to curve into trouble.
- *When a hazard runs across the fairway.* If a cross bunker or creek runs horizontally across the fairway, don't flirt with disaster by hitting the driver. Use the 3-wood, especially if you're playing a course for the first time.

There is nothing unique about the type of swing you make with the 3-wood. Play it just like the driver in terms of ball position. The only cautionary note has to do with the height you tee the ball. Never tee the ball so the majority of it rests higher than the top of the clubhead. The clubface of the 3-wood usually is shallower, or shorter from top to bottom, than the driver, and there's a danger that you'll undercut the ball and hit a pop-up. Tee the ball lower, so the top one-fourth of it is above the top of the clubhead.

THE ART OF
LAYING UP

So many amateurs are inconsistent with the quality of their club-ball contact, they don't control distances very well. As a result they don't think twice about their second shots on par-5 holes. They merely bash the ball as far as they can and wind up with a lot of awkward distances for their third shot. Belting the ball to within 50 yards of the green isn't always good because for most amateurs the 50-yard wedge shot is one of the most delicate in the game. It's hard to apply enough spin to the ball to make it stop close to the hole. If you have to shoot over a bunker to the flagstick, the task is even tougher.

I believe the lay-up second shot is one of the most overlooked in golf. When I think of good lay-up players, I think of Tom Kite. Tom is deadly with a sand wedge from distances between 80 and 100 yards, and on long par 5s he pays very close attention to his second shot so he leaves himself that perfect sand-wedge distance.

Thinking of Tom brings to mind Pebble Beach Golf Links, where he won the 1992 U.S. Open. The 18th hole there is one of the most famous holes in the world. It's a par 5 that requires a drive to the fairway and then a long second to a well-protected green. I seldom use a driver off the tee on that hole. I hit a 3-wood safely to the fairway, then hit maybe a 3-iron for my second shot. Under typical conditions, that strategy leaves me with 100 yards to the green—perfect wedge distance.

Talking about laying up on par 5s may seem odd in a discussion about fairway woods, and in truth it's one area where a fairway wood probably shouldn't be used at all. You should take note of the distance to the green—say it's 240 yards—and try to hit the ball 160 yards so you have that pet 80-yard distance left for your third shot (*4-10*). As a corollary to that, practice your 80-yard wedge shot often. It'll produce a lot of scoring opportunities for you.

CHOOSING THE RIGHT
FAIRWAY WOOD

When you go shopping for a fairway wood (or two or three), keep versatility in mind. I see too much emphasis on distance, too little on accuracy and the club's effectiveness from different lies. Experiment and find a model that performs well when the ball is in divots, tall grass and from the fairway. Don't necessarily go with the wood that hits the ball the far-

4-10: *When reaching the green on a par-5 hole is impossible, be intelligent with your lay-up second shot. Instead of blasting away to the awkward 50-yard distance, hit a controlled shot to your favorite distance—which for me is 80 yards.*

thest. Conduct a test where you hit 20 balls with each club you are trying out and choose the one that produces the tightest shot dispersion. Accuracy is more important than distance in a fairway wood.

If you haven't ventured into the world of 5-woods, 6-woods and even 7-woods, you should. They're extremely easy to hit from the fairway, but their real calling card is their effectiveness out of the rough. A wide number of models are available.

THREE NEAT SHOTS

1. Hitting out of a divot

Nobody is happy to find their perfect, center-cut drive lying in a divot. But there's a technique for playing from them that will help you achieve more distance than you might think.

The situation: You've boomed a big drive on a long par-4 hole and find your ball in a fresh, deep divot. You still have 185 yards to the

4-11: Playing out of a divot is similar to playing out of rough. Position the ball back in your stance and align your feet, hips and shoulders open to the left.

green. A long iron is out of the question because the rear portion of the divot is higher than the bottom portion of the ball and won't allow the you to slide the clubhead under the ball through impact. The 4-wood is the choice.

The setup: Line up for the shot similar to the way you play out of rough—ball back in your stance (*4-11*), your feet, hips and shoulders aligned to the left of the target. There's one more consideration: Choke down on the club about an inch. Because there isn't deep grass just in front of the ball, it will come out faster than a shot out of rough. Choking down will modify the total distance you get. Instead of your normal 210 yards, you've programmed the ball to go 185.

The swing: First, aim the leading edge of the fairway wood at the ball's equator. You don't want to hit behind the ball at all. Your thought is to hit down sharply on the ball and think of driving it right into the ground. You want to make the divot even deeper.

Your takeaway should be steep, the clubhead coming up quickly on the backswing. Allow your body to turn fully because it's a shot that requires speed and force. Slam the clubhead down into the back of the ball. Expect a lower trajectory and plenty of roll. In this case, the ball will fly 165 yards and roll 20 more after it lands—a perfect 185 yards.

2. From a fairway bunker

Few full-swing shots require as much creativity and sheer concentration as hitting a fairway wood from a bunker. You need to make several adjustments in your setup and substantially alter your swing. But if your lie is good, the fairway wood will produce some fantastic shots. If your ball is sitting down, though, forget it. Blast out to the fairway.

The situation: You've driven into a fairway bunker and have 190 yards left to the hole. The sand is firm and your ball is sitting up cleanly.

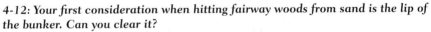

4-12: Your first consideration when hitting fairway woods from sand is the lip of the bunker. Can you clear it?

4-13: The standard fairway wood shot from sand. Align your feet, hips and shoulders open to the left, aiming the clubface at your target. Note that you should choke down on the club to compensate for shifting your feet into the sand.

A long iron is out of the question; if you hit behind the ball even a hair, you'll catch sand between the ball and clubface and dub the shot. Your first consideration is the lip of the bunker 10 yards in front of your ball *(4-12)*. Can you hit the ball high enough to clear it? You decide that a 4-wood will give you sufficient height to get the ball over the lip.

The setup: In Chapter 2 I explained that your stance width should never vary for full-swing shots. This shot is the only exception. You'll need to make a big swing, and for that you'll need extra stability in your lower body to maintain your footing. Widen your stance, so your feet are wider than the outside points of your shoulders. Your alignment is open, your feet and hips aiming to the left of the target line *(4-13)*. Grip the club after you've opened the clubface in relation to your stance.

Settle your feet into the sand. How deep you penetrate with your feet depends on the consistency of the sand; the softer the surface, the deeper you penetrate. On firm sand, settling your feet about an inch will do.

Now comes an important key: Because you settled your feet an inch into the sand, you've effectively placed the ball an inch above your feet. To compensate, you need to choke down on the club an inch as well. Now you are "measured off" correctly when you address the ball. Choking down also gives you more control of the club.

Because your lie is good, place the ball forward in your stance, off your left heel. You want to make a sweeping-type swing similar to a fairway wood shot.

The swing: This is a precision shot and you want to eliminate as much movement in your swing as you can. On the backswing, keep your feet and legs very quiet. Keep your cool. Don't let anxiety disrupt your tempo and rhythm. Think of swinging smoothly and hitting the ball cleanly. Don't try to help the ball in the air, just swing the clubhead level with the surface of the bunker through impact.

Now comes the payoff. Your ball flight will be no different than if you were hitting from the fairway, with the exception that the ball will fly a shorter distance due to your choking down on the club and restricting movement in your feet and legs. The ball also will stop quickly after landing. This shot was 190 yards, and if your standard 4-wood shot is 215 yards, you're right on the money.

3. The low wind-cheater from the fairway

On the 16th hole at Shinnecock during the last round of the U.S. Open, my second shot was a brute. The wind was dead in my face, and I needed as much distance as possible to leave me a short third shot. A standard 3-wood shot wouldn't do. The ball would have flown too high into that vicious headwind, and I would have been left with a full 6-iron, too much club to hit into that well-bunkered green. I didn't want to hit a driver, though, because that demanded too precise a swing.

I played the 3-wood, but deliberately hit the ball low. The shot bored through the wind and got to within 115 yards of the green. I hit an 8-iron for my third shot—that tells you how hard the wind was blowing—but playing a more lofted iron enabled me to hit the green easily

4-14: To keep the ball under the wind, you need to effectively deloft the clubface. The way to do that is to play the ball back in your stance, well to the right of center.

and have a chance at a birdie. The low wind-cheater from the fairway is a terrific shot to have in your arsenal, and it's as effective in crosswinds as it is hitting into headwinds.

The situation: You're playing a long par 5 where the fairway gets narrower as you get closer to the hole. The wind is blowing dead in your face at 25 m.p.h. You've hit a decent drive but are left with 270 yards to the green—an unattainable distance. But you want to get within 60 yards of the green for your third shot, and a standard 3-wood simply won't go 190 yards.

The setup: You want to hit the ball low to keep it under the wind, so you should position the ball to the right of center in your stance *(4-14)*. To further encourage a low, driving trajectory, you should also set up to play a slight draw. Align your feet, hips and shoulders at the right edge of the green and aim the clubface at the hole.

4-15: Compare this follow-through with my finish on other swings, and you'll see I've left more weight on my right side. To hit the low shot successfully, you don't want to shift your weight excessively to the left.

The swing: You've dialed in the low shot at address, so the important thing now is to trust that your setup will get the job done without tinkering with your swing. The tendency is to slide your body forward on the downswing in an effort to deloft the clubface. Stay on your right side a little longer than usual and keep your head still. On your follow-through, keep more weight on your right side than usual *(4-15)*, but make sure you've transferred some weight onto your left side. The shot will come out very low, will draw a hair to the left, and run a good ways after landing. You'll get that 190 yards with ease.

Chapter 5

THE IRON MAN

HAVING PLAYED GOLF ALMOST CONSTANTLY for more than 30 years, I think the fact that I no longer carry a 2-iron in my bag says something about the difficulty of hitting long irons well. Not that I can't hit a long-iron shot well when I have to—I clinched the 1994 Nissan Los Angeles Open thanks to a nice 2-iron approach to the last green. But the occasions when I needed to hit a 2-iron were so rare, and the club itself is so demanding to hit, I removed it from my bag prior to the 1995 season. The long irons, which I define as the 1- through 4-irons, are simply too much club for the average amateur to handle.

Today I use my 4-wood in most cases where a 2-iron is required. Using lofted fairway woods in lieu of long irons is a trend that's catching on at all levels of the game, particularly among high-handicappers. The addition of 4- and 5-woods to the set (and I see a lot of 7-woods in place of 4-irons, too) is the most significant equipment development in years.

The middle irons—which I define as the 5- and 6-irons—are no piece of cake, either. They present problems of a similar nature, though not as pronounced. I see very few amateurs who are good middle-iron players. When I refer to long irons in this chapter, the principles I discuss usually apply to the middle irons, too.

Before we move on to the technique for hitting long irons, I should describe their characteristics and why they are so difficult to hit.

- *They are simply longer than the other irons.* The farther the clubhead is from your hands, the more difficult it becomes to time impact so you hit the ball solidly with a square clubface.
- *They don't have as much loft.* It's extremely difficult to hit the ball high with a long or middle iron, simply because they have so little loft. The problem is similar to hitting a driver off the fairway—it can be done, but the quality of the shot usually isn't very good. When you have minimal loft, you need a great deal of clubhead speed to carry the ball the distance the irons were designed to produce.
- *They are unforgiving on off-center hits.* The sweet spot on low irons is the same size as the sweet spot on other clubs, but the clubhead is moving much faster at impact. The high clubhead speed and the longer swing required to produce it make it difficult to hit the ball right on the button every time. And, while an off-center hit on a 9-iron may cause you a five-yard loss of distance, an off-center hit with a 2-iron can cost you 15 yards or more. That's a high price to pay.
- *You need an excellent lie to hit them solidly.* Long irons aren't very versatile. They are difficult out of the rough. They aren't very effective from divots or when the ball is sitting down. It's difficult to alter the ball's trajectory, too, at least when you need to hit the ball higher than normal. The average player needs a near-perfect lie to use them effectively.
- *They require strength and superb hand-eye coordination.* The best long-iron player I've seen was Jack Nicklaus in his prime. Jack had extraordinary physical strength. He also swung the club into the ball on a fairly steep angle but at the same time didn't take much of a divot. It is extremely difficult to swing the club in this manner. The middle-irons are much more manageable because they don't demand as upright a swing.

These considerations notwithstanding, long and middle irons are useful, and the fundamentals required to play them are the same as for the other clubs. If you use fairway woods in place of long irons, you do leave yourself at a certain disadvantage. Generally, a long iron struck well flies a bit lower than the fairway wood you'd use in its place, and the long iron generally holds its line better in the wind.

The advantages of a purely struck long iron are illustrated by my experience in the final round of the 1994 Nissan Los Angeles Open at Riviera Country Club. I came to the 18th hole with a two-stroke lead over Fred Couples and hit a good drive into the fairway. The 18th is uphill all the way, which makes it play very long. My drive left me with more than 200 yards to the green, but hitting a fairway wood was a poor option because I would have had to make a short, easy swing. I wanted to make a full, aggressive swing because my adrenaline was really pumping. I chose my 2-iron.

I had a sidehill lie with the ball below my feet. It's difficult to draw the ball from that type of lie and I didn't want to hit a draw anyway because the trouble was to the left of the green. I elected to play a fade, the ball starting at the hole and curving slightly to the right where I had lots of green to work with. I aligned my feet and shoulders slightly to the left of the hole and aimed the clubface dead at the flagstick. I played the ball an inch farther back in my stance than normal and just made an aggressive but unhurried swing. The ball took off like a bullet, landed just short of the green and bounded up 40 feet from the hole. I two-putted for the victory.

An iron shot from the middle of the fairway that stops 40 feet from the hole isn't so spectacular, I guess. But it proves two things: (a) that a long-iron can be useful in certain situations, and (b) I haven't hit a lot of memorable long-iron shots in my career. Like I said, they're the hardest clubs in the bag to hit close to the hole.

LONG IRONS
TAKE LONGER

Amateurs share several common mechanical flaws with their long-iron play, but those flaws are rooted in the same basic problem: fear and anxiety. When amateurs stand over a long-iron shot, they are besieged with a who-am-I-kidding sense that they're likely to fail. That attitude makes one of the hardest shots in golf even more difficult. The lack of confidence results in a hurried swing. Watching high-handicappers swing, it's almost like they can't wait to get the shot over with. They swing much too fast, particularly on the backswing and on the first move down. Timing is disrupted, there's no flow to the swing, and all effort is wasted. A fast swing is usually a short swing, and if there's one thing you must do with a long iron, it's make a longer, rhythmic swing.

Before we get into details about the mechanics of the swing, remember that first lesson: Calm down. Take your time. Relax your muscles. Long irons take longer to happen, so ease off and allow the swing to happen.

BALL POSITION
IS CRITICAL

The setup for the long irons is the same as for the other clubs, except that you should move the ball farther forward in your stance. You want to play the ball inside your left heel with the 2-iron and about 1½ inches or so back as you progress through the other irons. Because the long irons don't have a lot of loft, moving the ball forward in your stance allows you to take full advantage of the loft they do have. Changing your ball position is much better than trying to create loft by hitting up on the ball or positioning your hands behind the ball at address.

LET THE CLUB
DO THE WORK

Long irons are intimidating to look at. Their appearance gives the impression you have to inject something extra into the swing in order to make the shot come off well. That isn't the case. The same smooth, unhurried pass you make with other clubs will produce fine shots, provided your technique is good. To that end, I suggest you take one club more than normal for every shot with a long iron. If it looks like a 4-iron shot, hit the 3-iron instead. This will take a lot of pressure off you.

Psychologically you'll be more likely to swing smoothly and concentrate on hitting the ball solidly.

Of course, by taking one more club you may be concerned about hitting the ball too low to achieve maximum carry. Unless you have to fly the ball over a greenside bunker, don't worry about it. Let the ball land short of the green and bounce forward. The shot may not look majestic, but the net distance the ball travels will be about the same.

FADE THE BALL
WHENEVER POSSIBLE

It's easier to hit the ball high when you fade the ball. By opening your stance and aiming the clubface at the target, you effectively increase the club's loft. It's an efficient way of turning a 2-iron into a 3-iron. What's more, the fade swing increases the odds of hitting the ball solidly. The clubhead's angle of descent into the ball is a bit steeper, which decreases the odds of hitting the shot fat.

5-1: Setting up open will make your long-iron play immeasurably easier because, in effect, you are increasing the club's loft.

5-2: On the downswing and into the follow-through, work your right shoulder under your chin. This will help you swing the shoulders along a uniform plane back and through, which in turn makes it easier to hit the ball solidly.

Start by setting up open, your feet and hips aligned left of the target (5-1). From this position two swing thoughts will help you produce a dependable fade. The first is to try to work your right shoulder down and under your chin on the downswing and into your follow-through (5-2). Feel as though your right shoulder is moving toward the ground. This encourages your shoulders to turn on the plane you established at address and helps you maintain the open clubface through impact.

Second, make sure the heel of the club arrives at impact before the toe of the club. That will insure an open clubface and a left-to-right ball flight. The idea is to curb clubface rotation. If you fan the clubface closed on the downswing and the toe arrives at the ball before the heel, the clubface will be closed and you'll pull the ball to the left.

The fade swing works for virtually any club, but the draw swing does not. With the long irons, I discourage you from even trying to draw the ball. The tendency is to either (a) smother the ball by trying to rotate the clubface closed through impact or (b) hit it thin and to the right by trying to stay behind the ball at impact. It takes years of practice and lots of talent to hit a high draw with a long iron. In fact, it's the hardest shot in golf.

The middle irons are different. They are short enough and have enough loft to permit a deliberate draw. It takes practice, though. If you're an advanced player, there is one thought that will help you shape the shot from right to left: Stand tall at address and stay that way through impact. The taller you stand, the easier it becomes to turn the clubface over through impact.

Regardless of the direction you are trying to curve the ball, one principle must be adhered to: The left wrist must be flat at impact. Breaking down with the left wrist—letting it hinge so it forms a cup—is one of the most serious errors in golf. It results from the right hand overpowering the left, and it not only changes the direction the clubface aims, but it adds unwanted loft to the clubface. It's also a sign of deceleration, a killer of golf shots.

SWEEP THE BALL
OFF THE GROUND

With the short irons and even the fairway woods, it's sometimes advisable to hit down sharply on the ball and take a good-sized divot. That technique doesn't work very well with the long and middle irons. First, hitting down on the ball is only effective when your ball is positioned back in your stance, and you want the ball forward for the longer irons. Second, hitting down on the ball usually produces a lower ball flight, and with the long irons especially, you don't need to make the ball fly any lower than what their low loft already will produce.

Through impact, you want to take a marginal divot, sometimes no divot at all. You just want to shave the blades of grass off near their base. The turf should have a shredded appearance directly underneath the ball after it is gone. To accomplish this, you need a very shallow angle of approach with the clubhead through impact. To ingrain that sensation, practice swinging the club back until your hands are at hip height and swinging through so your hands finish at hip height on the follow-through. Imagine that the swing arc of the clubhead is saucer-shaped, rather than bowl-shaped. The key is to keep the clubhead low to the ground before and after impact.

KEEP YOUR HEAD DOWN
THROUGH IMPACT

Anxiety tends to make golfers "peek" too soon in their urgency to see where the ball went. With the long and middle irons, it's a fatal mistake. When your head rises, your body rises along with it. That causes the clubhead to come up abruptly even before you strike the ball. All kinds

5-3: A subtle but dangerous tendency with long irons is to lift your head too soon in your eagerness to see how the shot turned out. A key thought is to keep your head down through impact, refusing to look up until well after the ball is gone.

of mis-hits can result, although it usually produces thin shots. You want to stay down on the shot until after the ball is gone (5-3). My key for almost all full shots—straightening the right arm through impact—works wonderfully here.

CLUB SELECTION: BEWARE OF THE 10-YARD RULE

Years ago, somebody came up with the idea that each successive iron in your bag should produce 10 more yards of carry. It's a foolish "rule" that has seduced many amateurs. In truth, the 10-yard rule applies only to stronger players with high swing speeds. If you hit an 8-iron 140 yards through the air, it may very well be that you carry the 7-iron 150 yards and the 6-iron 160 yards. From there, the 10-yard rule starts to disintegrate. The 5-iron that should carry 170 yards typically only flies 165 yards. By the time you get to the 3-iron, which by the 10-yard rule should carry 190 yards, you find the rule doesn't apply at all. Not only do you misjudge the distance the ball carries, you may swing too aggressively in your effort to get the distance you "should" be getting.

To determine your individual distances, there is no alternative but to go to the practice range and note how far you actually carry the ball with each club. I recommend actually pacing off the yardage—most pros do. You might be surprised at what you find, and it will make you a much smarter player.

Club selection is critical. Raw distance isn't the only factor involved in choosing the right "weapon." There are many other considerations, including:

- *Temperature.* The colder the air is, the shorter the ball flies. Even if you keep your golf balls in your pocket to keep them warm, they still won't fly as far in cold air.
- *Wind.* Obviously, the ball doesn't go as far when you're hitting into a headwind. What not many amateurs know is, the ball doesn't fly as far hitting downwind either, unless you really hit the ball high. As for crosswinds, the effect on distance depends on the direction

the wind is blowing and the direction you're curving the ball. If you're fading the ball into a right-to-left crosswind, the wind will take distance off the shot. The same is true when drawing the ball into a left-to-right wind, though it won't take as much off the shot because of the piercing quality of the draw.

Wind is a big factor in golf, so it pays to know which way it's blowing. But wind direction can be deceiving and difficult to determine. If you're playing a course with lots of trees, the air can be still at ground level but howling above the treetops—which is where the ball will often be at the apex of its flight. Moreover, trees and valleys can deflect wind currents and give a false sense of which way the wind is blowing. A perfect example is the par-3 12th hole at Augusta National, home of the Masters. Though only a 155-yard hole, it's one of the trickiest in the world because the wind swirls and its true direction is very hard to determine.

There are some shrewd tricks to determining wind direction. Look at the tops of trees to see which way the wind is making them lean. If you're near a body of water, watch the direction of the waves. Also look for the calmest area of the lake or pond—the wind is blowing away from the calm water. Also, watch the clouds—provided they're low in the sky. Don't trust cloud movement at high altitudes.

- *Altitude.* If you're used to playing at sea level, get ready for an ego-building surprise when you tee it up in the mountains. The air is thinner and the ball flies farther. Depending on the altitude, it can make a two-club difference in the distance you carry the ball.

STRATEGY FOR DIFFERENT
GREEN ELEVATIONS

If your standard 5-iron distance is 155 yards, that distance only holds true if your ball and the green are at the same elevation. But few golf courses are perfectly flat. Most of them have greens that are above or slightly below the fairway. The elevation of the green has a profound effect on distance.

Elevated greens increase the effective yardage of the shot. A 155-yard shot to an elevated green can play 10 yards or more longer. Only experience can train your eye to discern how much longer it will play. Generally, elevated greens are more difficult to approach than greens that are below you. The ball will approach the green on a shallower angle, so it doesn't land as softly. The shot that lands on the front of the green may very well wind up in the back.

Playing elevated greens requires shrewd judgment. The main consideration is the hole location. If the flagstick is on the front part of the green, it's best to take more club and risk hitting the ball a bit long. Don't gamble and try to hit a precise shot that lands on the front part of the green short of the flagstick. If you miss the shot even a little, you'll be short of the green and you'll have a difficult uphill chip shot. (Most elevated greens have rough short of the putting surface.) If you hit long, however, you'll usually have a simple chip shot with plenty of green to work with. My basic rule is this: If you can see half the flagstick or more from the fairway, assume the flagstick is up and take plenty of club. If only the flag itself is exposed, you also should take plenty of club so you can get the ball back to the hole.

If the green is below you, hit less club. The ball will stay in the air longer and carry forward farther. Because your ball has more "hang time," it is affected more by the wind. The trick is to get the ball on the ground as soon as possible by hitting a lower shot. Take less club and play the ball back in your stance.

THE DREADED "FLYER" LIE

One of the scariest shots in golf occurs when your ball is nestled in grass that isn't so deep as to make you flub the shot completely, but deep enough that grass will get caught between the ball and clubface at impact. It's called a "flyer" lie, and it's one of the most unpredictable shots in the game.

Sometimes you'll hit behind the ball and catch too much grass between the ball and clubface, robbing your shot of yardage. A 160-yard shot might go only 140 yards. In contrast, if you hit the ball as purely as possible and a small amount of grass gets between the ball and club-face, the opposite may occur: The grass acts as a lubricant and the ball "jumps" off the clubface with hardly any backspin. It flies farther than normal—the 160-yard shot might carry 170 yards—and the ball air-mails the green.

I've discovered a technique for playing the flyer that's almost fool-proof. The secret is to select one club more than what you'd use if the lie were perfect and to aim the leading edge of the clubface at the ball's

5-4, 5-5: When hitting middle irons from rough, aim the leading edge of the club-face at the ball's equator (left). On the backswing, take the clubhead back low and level with the turf (right), to promote a sweeping-type blow through impact.

equator (5-4). Instead of hitting down sharply on the ball in an attempt to dig it out of the grass, sweep the ball from its lie. Take the club back low and slow (5-5) and swing through so the clubhead is moving parallel with the ground through impact. If you contact the ball at its equator, very little grass will get caught between the clubhead and the ball. What's more, you aren't squashing the ball flush against the clubface because you're hitting it with the leading edge. It's a thin shot, played deliberately.

The ball will come out a bit lower than usual and won't fly as far as a shot from a good lie. You won't get a lot of backspin either, but the ball will land softly and roll forward toward the hole.

ALWAYS TEE BALL
ON PAR 3s

When asked why he tees the ball on par-3 holes rather than play directly off the turf, Jack Nicklaus once replied, "I discovered long ago that air

5-6: On par-3 holes, tee the ball so the center of the clubface is slightly below the ball's equator.

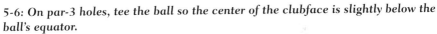

offers less resistance than dirt." I couldn't agree more. Always tee the ball on par 3s. Take advantage of the opportunity to create a perfect lie for yourself.

The trick is to tee the ball the correct height. In my opinion, most amateurs tee the ball too high. This causes you to either hit up on the ball through impact or, if you hit down on the ball correctly, to strike the ball too high on the clubface. You should tee the ball so the ball's equator is slightly higher than the center point of the clubface (5-6). That way, you can still make a descending blow and not risk undercutting the ball.

5-7—5-10: Your first option from 160 yards is the easiest. Align your feet and shoulders square to the target and make your normal swing, concentrating on turning your shoulders fully on the backswing. A full turn will help you take the clubhead back inside the target line, and on the downswing you should swing the clubhead into the ball on the same path. Finish with a full, free follow-through.

THREE NEAT SHOTS—
ALL FROM 160 YARDS

To be a good shotmaker, you need to be able to play different shots from the same distance. Conditions such as wind, green elevation, hole location and ground are important factors in determining the type of shot you want to hit. It may be a low shot, a fade or draw, or even a run-up shot. Here are three options for playing the same shot from the same distance.

1. The standard 6-iron

For me, 160 yards is standard distance for a medium 6-iron; yours may differ. When wind and other adverse conditions aren't present, play the ball just to the left of center of your stance and align your feet and shoulders parallel to the target line (5-7). Swing the club back slightly to the inside, letting your wrists break naturally just before your hands reach hip-height. Turn your shoulders fully with the club almost reaching par-

allel at the top (5-8). On the downswing and through impact, swing the clubhead along your stance line (5-9), the same way you took the club back. Let the momentum of the swing carry you into a full, free finish (5-10). This all-purpose 6-iron will hit the green on the fly and settle quickly after landing.

2. Hard draw with a 7-iron

If there's no obstacle short and right of the green, and the hole is located on the back-left portion of the green, you might choose to hit a low draw that lands on the front part of the green and releases toward the

5-11—5-14: The advantage of drawing the ball on your approach is that the ball will roll a ways after landing, perfect when the flagstick is in the rear portion of the green. Align your feet and shoulders to the right, aim the clubface at the hole, and swing the club back and through along your stance line. Remember to keep your head down through impact and beyond.

hole. It's a better option than trying to fly the ball back to the hole because the high-flying shot too often ends up long or short.

Align your feet and shoulders to the right side of the green, but aim the clubface at the flagstick. Make sure you grip the club after you've aimed the clubface. Take the club back well to the inside (5-11), as you'll want to swing down along an inside path. Turn your shoulders as far as comfortably possible so you are fully coiled at the top of your backswing (5-12). Swing down from the inside (5-13) and concentrate on letting the clubhead follow your body lines. Keep your head down through impact and beyond (5-14), as that will help you hit the ball solidly and keep the clubface sufficiently delofted to produce a low ball flight. The ball should start to the right of the green and then swing to the left, hitting the front part of the green and skidding back to the hole.

5-15—5-18: The low punch is effective when you want to keep the ball under the wind. Play the ball back in your stance, shorten your backswing and hit down firmly on the ball. Keep your follow-through fairly short so it comes close to matching your abbreviated turn on the backswing.

3. Punch shot with a 5-iron

If the wind is blowing hard in your face, there are no obstacles short of the green and the turf is firm, the low punch shot is extremely effective. You see this type of shot played a lot during the British Open. The idea is to hit the ball 160 yards on the fly, then let it run the remaining 10 onto the green. Once you get the hang of it, it's a much better choice than hitting a higher shot that's at the mercy of the wind.

You're deliberately playing a low shot, so position the ball just to the right of center in your stance (5-15). Don't play the ball farther back

than that, though. It isn't necessary because the loft of the 5-iron is low for a shot of this length. Make a shorter backswing than with a full shot (5-16), but don't deliberately omit any part of your body from the swing. You want your hips and shoulders to turn, just not as much. Through impact, keep your head down until after the ball is gone (5-17).

The real key to the punch shot is your follow-through. Even before you begin the swing, think of keeping your follow-through short (5-18). Long follow-throughs are for longer shots.

Chapter 6

ZEROING IN WITH
SHORT IRONS

MY PHILOSOPHY WITH THE LONGER CLUBS is to keep the ball in play so I can avoid making bogeys. I expect accuracy from my driver, fairway woods and long irons, but I seldom expect pinpoint precision. Shots with the longer clubs cover too much distance to hit the ball within six feet of where you're aiming. So if my drive curves 10 yards more to the right than I planned, fine. I'm still in position for par and maybe even a birdie.

The short irons are quite a different thing. The 7-, 8-, 9-iron and pitching wedge are scoring clubs that I hold to a much higher standard. With the longer clubs, I'm seldom aggressive. With the short irons, I go at the flag whenever I can. I expect to hit the ball close enough to the hole to have a very good chance of making the putt. In the end, it's your play with the short irons that determines whether you shoot a mediocre score or a good one. Even if your putting isn't sharp, if you hit the ball close enough, often enough, you'll hole your share of putts and shoot a good score.

Why are my expectations so high? The short irons are shorter in length, so the clubhead describes a much shorter arc from start to finish. The clubhead is nearer your hands as well, so you have more control of the clubface at impact. Your odds of hitting the ball solidly are increased enormously.

Then there is the design of the clubhead itself. The increased loft produces more height on the shot and more backspin, so you can pretty much count on the ball stopping close to where it lands. Increased loft also means less sidespin, so the ball won't hook or slice as much. If your swing path is consistent, it's easier to start the ball on the intended line of play.

The increased margin for error allows you to be more aggressive. That was my attitude on the par-5 18th hole at Weston Hills Country Club in the last round of the 1992 Honda Classic. I had double-bogeyed the 15th hole and bogeyed the 17th to fall out of the lead. A good drive and second shot at the 18th left me with 136 yards to the hole. I honestly thought I didn't have much of a chance of winning, but I desperately wanted to make a birdie so I at least would have a better finish.

A lake fronts that 18th green and the flagstick was in the front. If I chose to go at the hole, there would be almost no margin for error. My caddie, Eric Schwarz, gave me the yardage: 136 exactly to the hole. I needed to hit the ball as high as possible and contemplated hitting a hard 9-iron. I asked Eric for his opinion.

"You'd have to kill it to get it there," he said.

"Do you like a cut 8-iron better?" I asked.

"I like that a *lot* better," he said.

I decided I liked the 8-iron, too. If I hit the shot long, I'd still have a 10-footer down the hill for the birdie. If I missed it slightly, I'd still be over the water.

I aligned my feet and shoulders open and positioned the ball in the middle of my stance—I didn't want to force a higher trajectory by placing the ball farther forward. I aimed the clubface at the hole and then re-gripped the club. I swung firmly and kept my head down to guarantee solid contact.

The shot looked good in the air, and when the ball came down it just disappeared. It had flown directly into the hole for an eagle 3. I held my breath for a second because a ball that lands squarely in the hole often will pop out. When the ball stayed in, I went crazy. I threw my hat in the air, jumped around and gave Eric a high-five.

The eagle put me in a playoff against Fred Couples, and I won the tournament with a 15-foot putt on the second playoff hole.

I put two principles of shotmaking to good use on that 8-iron shot. When in doubt take plenty of club, and under pressure don't try to force a shot. It was as good a shot as I've ever hit.

RELAX RIGHT ARM, FIRM UP YOUR LEFT

I keep hammering home my principle that the true fundamentals don't change from club to club, and that certainly holds true with the short irons. But because I never intend to hit the ball a long way with the short irons, I concentrate on the factors that determine precision. My grip and posture have to be sound. I want my alignment to be perfect. And I make a couple of minor adjustments in my setup that guarantee my starting the ball dead on line with the flagstick.

To control distance well, your arms must be relaxed at address. Tension in the arms not only alters mechanics, it changes your tension level dramatically. If your arms are tight, they won't swing freely and you'll employ too much body motion to compensate. So I want my arms to feel limp and sensitive at address.

Both arms must be so relaxed that they hang vertically from your shoulder sockets at address. With the driver, your arms should extend slightly toward the ball. With the 8-iron, however, your arms should hang almost straight down.

When you complete the procedure of addressing the ball, your right arm should be bent slightly at the elbow (6-1). If your right arm is straight, you either are standing too far from the ball to accommodate the upright lie of the 8-iron, or there's too much tension. The tip of your right elbow should point at your right hip. That way, your right arm will fold naturally on the backswing. When you relax the right arm and let it bend, your right shoulder will relax and lower itself. It's a good sensation. Your upper body will feel tension-free and ready to swing.

6-1: At address your right arm should be relaxed and bent slightly at the elbow.

The left arm should be more rigid than the right and should be perpendicular to the ground (6-2). The left arm controls the arc of the swing and therefore must be kept fairly straight throughout the swing. If it feels loose and limp, it will collapse at the top of the swing. Keep the left arm straight, but don't lock it at the elbow.

BEND MORE
FROM THE HIPS

Posture is a true fundamental. You always want to bend over at the hips in order to get the club behind the ball. Because the 8-iron is shorter

6-2: *With the short irons, your left arm should hang vertically at address. It should remain straight and firm throughout the swing.*

than the driver, you may need to increase the amount of bending at the waist in order to reach the ball. But you should never compensate by bending at the waist because that gives your back a curved appearance and it won't rotate efficiently on the backswing. Never increase the flex of your knees either because that stifles turning with the upper body. You'll slide laterally instead, which destroys power and decreases the odds of making solid contact. Stand as tall as possible and seat the club comfortably behind the ball by bending from the hips.

CHOOSE AN
INTERMEDIATE TARGET

This is a device I use with all my clubs, but it's especially important with the short irons. Although the target is less than 150 yards away, that's a lot of distance between you and the hole. When you stand behind your ball at address, pick an object such as an old divot or a weed that is directly between your ball and your target. (In photo 6-3 I've substituted a headcover in place of an old divot for better recognition.) The idea is to make your ball fly over that intermediate target. If it does, the ball will fly directly at the hole.

An intermediate target simplifies your alignment procedure enormously. If you line up in relation to the intermediate target, it will help you line up correctly. It's also useful because you don't need to swivel

6-3: Choosing an intermediate target and making your ball fly directly over it is an effective way to start the ball on the correct line. The headcover I'm using here shows up better than an old divot or a discoloration in the turf.

your head back and forth to find the flagstick when you settle over the ball at address. All you need to do is shift your eyes and you'll find your intermediate target. From there, make your ball fly over the target.

YARDAGE TO HOLE DETERMINES
SIZE OF SWING

Some golfers don't decide how hard to hit the ball until they've settled in at address. It's a faulty procedure. You'll have much better luck if you imagine the force of the swing while you stand behind the ball during your preshot routine. Trajectory, ball position, shot shape and other factors should be visualized before you actually get over the ball. It's OK to fine-tune your waggle so you can hit the ball exactly the distance you desire. But the process should begin before you set up.

The entire club selection procedure should be done as early as possible. If you're in between clubs and aren't sure which one will get the job done, eliminate one by one the clubs you *don't* want to hit until you zero in on the right choice. If you're still in a quandary, go with more club. It's much more difficult to hit a hard 9-iron than an easy 8-iron. More often than not, hitting more club is the right choice to begin with.

WAGGLE TRIGGERS
THE SWING

Unlike other sports, golf is played from a static start. One moment you're standing motionless over the ball, the next moment every part of your body is in motion. It's very difficult to establish rhythm and tempo in your swing without some type of motion to get you started.

That's where the waggle comes in. The waggle is nothing more than a trigger that initiates the backswing. I don't recommend a specific type of waggle because it's highly individual. It can be performed with the legs—Gary Player kicks his right knee in toward the target just before taking the club back. Fuzzy Zoeller shoves the clubhead away from him so the ball is played off the heel of his club. Peter Jacobsen makes a funny little movement with his left foot. Jack Nicklaus swivels his head to the right. I like to rock back and forth between my left and right foot, then push my left hip forward.

These are examples of waggles that signal to your body that you're ready to start the backswing. I make no provisions for the waggle except to say that it should not dramatically alter your address position. If you waggle by shoving your hands toward the target, for example, you may change the relationship between the clubface and the target. The waggle should be a slight movement, that's all. Refine your waggle so it acts as a trigger mechanism, nothing more.

AVOID THE
THREE-QUARTER SWING

One of the most devilish tasks in golf is to try to hit your clubs a distance shorter than they were designed to produce. If you hit an 8-iron 140 yards but for some reason feel the need to make it fly only 125, you've got a job to do. It's much easier to make a full swing and make that 8-iron go 140 yards. When you try to lessen the distance the ball flies by shortening your swing, you're asking for trouble. It's much better to make an easier swing using your normal full-swing motion without decelerating before impact. It helps to understand that you can make a full swing and vary the distance of your short irons by as much as 15 yards. All you need to do is slow down the pace of your swing and accelerate the club a little more slowly through impact.

Understand, the swing with a short iron isn't a long swing to begin with. If you observe the best PGA Tour players in action, you'll notice that they swing their driver back to parallel at the top of the backswing, sometimes even farther. Their short-iron swing is naturally shorter. The problem comes when you try to shorten a swing that is already short to begin with. It's very difficult to sense exactly where your backswing should end, and your body parts don't fire in correct sequence. Your tempo is disrupted as well. You're likely to start down with a sudden jerk instead of changing direction smoothly and leisurely. So a longer swing is better.

If you find it difficult to make a longer, softer swing, try choking

6-4: *Choking down on the club is a great way to reduce your normal distance. Remember, choking down will make the ball fly lower than usual.*

down on the club an inch (6-4) and making your normal full swing. The ball will fly about the same distance as the longer club but will come out lower. You'll have plenty of control over the shot because the club is effectively lighter and the arc is narrower.

KEEP YOUR LOWER BODY QUIET

Because you aren't making a long swing with lots of motion, you want to restrict movement in your lower body during the swing. Too much leg and foot action will affect your balance just enough to cause you to hit

6-5, 6-6: Hitting balls with your feet together will train you to swing primarily with your upper body, a must on short-iron shots. Try to maintain your balance from start to finish.

the ball fat, thin or off-line. You want to feel like you're swinging the club with your hands, arms, shoulders and hips only. Don't worry about losing power. You'll find that your improved tempo and solid ball striking will produce more distance than an all-out, helter-skelter swing.

To train your lower body to remain passive during the swing, practice hitting balls with your feet together (6-5, 6-6). Don't move your feet at all and make sure they remain planted together well into your follow-through. There's no better drill for balance and for learning the correct motion with your upper body.

THE ALL-IMPORTANT
TRANSITION MOVE

The most critical part of the swing is the first move down from the top of the backswing. After you've swung the club back as far as you comfortably can, your swing has to change direction. This isn't as easy as it sounds. If the first move down is too fast, you expend too much energy too early and you won't hit the ball with authority. A sudden move down from the top destroys good mechanics, too. You may swing "over the top," or throw the club outside the target line. You might uncock your wrists too early. You may not shift your weight to the left correctly. Those are the major problems—there are many others.

The downswing should begin slowly. It should feel like a fluid continuation of the swing, which in fact it is. There is no need to rush because your power is applied late in the downswing anyway.

The key to a smooth transition is rhythm and tempo. Every good player has it. Some players may swing faster than others, but the speed of their swings is well-proportioned. It's like some inner clock directs the whole swing. To improve your tempo and your change of direction from the top, try dividing the swing into two segments. When you hit balls on the practice range, count "1" as you perform the backswing. Say it out loud—quietly, but out loud. Midway through the downswing, count "2." Do this over and over, forgetting swing mechanics and simply stressing the 1-2 cadence of your swing. The improved rhythm will have a profound impact on the consistency of your ball striking.

HIP-TO-HIP SWINGS
IMPROVE CLUBFACE CONTROL

The closer you are to the green, the more important direction control becomes. The drive that strays 10 yards off line is still playable. The short iron that sails 10 yards off line often is not. Bunkers, water, tall grass and certain bogeys await. The primary determinant of direction control is the position of the clubface at impact. If the clubface is open or closed by only a few degrees, the shot can be ruined completely.

You don't want to try to force the clubface into a square position at impact. It's far too stressful to even try. Tension will creep into your swing, your muscles will tighten and you'll lose control over distance. What's more, the clubface is tearing through the air so fast through impact that to try to guide the clubface into a perfectly square position is just about impossible.

The clubface should square naturally through impact as the result of a good grip and efficient hand action. If your fundamentals are sound at address, the clubface will return to impact the way you programmed it at the start. You should let your hands rotate easily through impact to the square position you desire.

An effective way to train your hands to perform correctly is to make short swings without a ball. Assume your address position and then swing the club back to hip height. Keeping your hands and arms relaxed, fluidly swing the club through the hitting area, brushing the top of the grass. Terminate the swing when your hands reach hip height on the follow-through. Do this over and over, perhaps 20 times. Your back-swing and follow-through should be mirror images of each other (6-7, 6-8), with the right arm folding on the backswing, the left arm folding on the follow-through. Feel your wrists uncocking smoothly through impact. As you acquire the knack of letting the clubface square natural-ly through impact, you'll find your short irons flying straighter—and far-ther, too.

HOW TO READ
YOUR DIVOTS

The divots you take with a short iron are deeper than with the long and middle irons because you want to hit down firmly on the ball in order to impart backspin. Your divots are like a road map that tells you what type of swing you made. If your divots are deep, your swing probably is too upright. Chances are you aren't turning your shoulders level on the backswing. Your left shoulder is probably dipping down dramatically instead of staying just slightly below your right shoulder. Deep divots usually come from an outside-to-inside swing path as well. Practice

6-7, 6-8: When you swing primarily with your upper body, the task of squaring the clubface through impact falls to your hands. Making hip-to-hip practice swings will train you to use your hands and wrists correctly.

swinging the clubhead into the ball from inside the target line. Your angle of approach will be shallower and your divots will become less deep and more uniform.

Ideally, your divot should occur immediately in front of the ball. The clubhead should strike the ball as it moves downward through impact, then continue downward until it takes a strip of turf from the ground. The deepest part of the divot should be just ahead of where the front of the ball was at address.

Your divots should aim right along the line you want the ball to start on. If you examine the teeing ground of any par 3, you'll notice that most divots point just to the left of the green. Don't assume this is the proper way to take divots. What you're observing is the tendency of most amateurs to cut across the ball from outside to in.

The depth of your divots isn't the only giveaway of a poor swing.

The uniformity of the divot itself tells you a lot about your equipment, setup at address and your hand action through the ball. If your divot is deeper on the side nearest you, then the heel of the club is digging deeper than the toe. This is a common cause of pulled shots to the left because when the club is set on its heel, you are effectively aiming the clubface to the left of the target. It may be that your clubs are too upright or that you're carrying your hands too low at address. It's impossible for me to tell without seeing you swing, but a PGA professional will be able to tell you the nature of your problem.

Without getting into too much detail about your equipment, it's important that your clubs have the correct lie for your height and build. To determine the correct lie, assume your address position on a cart path or bare floor. The entire sole of the club should not rest flush against the ground. The portion of the sole out near the toe should be slightly off the ground because on the downswing, centrifugal force causes the clubshaft to droop downward, seating the sole of the club perfectly.

REMEDY FOR
FAT SHOTS

Few shots are as maddening as the fat shot, when you strike the ground behind the ball. At best you achieve only glancing club-ball contact because the clubhead bounces off the turf and into the ball. At worst, the divot is so deep it destroys clubhead speed completely and the divot flies farther than the ball. Fat shots can be caused by standing too close to the ball. But usually they are due to tilting your left shoulder sharply downward on the backswing instead of turning it under your chin in a more level manner.

A proven cure for tilting your shoulders instead of turning them is to practice hitting a ball from a sidehill lie with the ball above your feet (6-9). If your left shoulder moves directly downward on the backswing, it has to rise up on the forward swing. That produces a very steep angle of approach with the clubhead bottoming out well behind the ball. If you tilt your left shoulder from a sidehill lie, you'll hit as much as a foot behind the ball and won't move it forward at all. To make clean club-

6-9: A chief cause of fat shots is tilting your shoulders instead of turning them. A sure cure is to practice hitting balls from a side-hill lie with the ball above your feet. That forces you to turn your shoulders level, back and through.

ball contact, you are forced to turn your shoulders level on the backswing. Practice this drill regularly, and you'll hit the ball more solidly with all your clubs.

REMEDY FOR
THIN SHOTS

When your divots are too deep, your clubhead is approaching the ball on too steep an angle. With thin shots, the opposite is true. The clubhead bottoms out behind the ball, then is traveling upward when it

6-10—6-14: A five-step drill to learn the correct weight shift on the downswing. As you stride through on the downswing, be conscious of the pushing action with your right foot onto your left leg. At the finish, most of your weight should be on your left side.

strikes the ball. Thin shots can occur when you stand too far from the ball. But usually they are due to poor transfer of weight from your right side to the left on the downswing. Your weight shifts to your right side on the backswing, but then stays there on the way down.

To improve your weight shift and eliminate thin shots, practice the following drill. Start with your normal address position *(6-10)*, then draw your left foot back until it touches your right foot *(6-11)*. Swing to the top, keeping your feet together *(6-12)*. Then, on the downswing, stride to the left with your left foot and hit the ball *(6-13, 6-14)*. Only if you drive off your right foot and shift your weight to the left will you be able to make clean contact. It's a wonderful drill for the practice range.

NEAT SHOT:
THE KNOCKDOWN

Shots with the short irons fly high and stay in the air a long time. That makes them more susceptible to crosswinds that can blow the ball off line. Headwinds will decrease carry and make the ball behave different- ly when it strikes the green. Playing downwind is treacherous, too. If you hit the ball high, the ball will simply ride the wind and carry too far. What's more, the ball will come down "hot" and backspin is negated. If you're a natural low-ball hitter, hitting downwind can work the other way. The wind can actually decrease carry distance because the wind won't let the ball climb to the peak of its trajectory.

Wind is the single biggest outside factor in the game, and the role it plays in short-iron play is more significant than with the other clubs. Efforts to minimize the effect of wind led to the most amazing shot in the modern pro's repertory: The low "knockdown" shot that appears to be oblivious to the wind and brakes to a quick halt shortly after hitting the green. It's one of the most useful shotmaking tools in golf and one of the easiest to execute.

The situation: The wind is gusting 20 m.p.h. on a straightaway par-5 hole, and two big shots have left you with 115 yards to the center of the green. There is water in front of the green and bunkers left and right. Your normal 9-iron distance is 130 yards, but you've ruled out a

6-15, 6-16: To play the the knockdown shot, position the ball well to the right of center in your stance. Because control is more important than distance, shorten your backswing.

normal 9-iron for this shot because the wind is gusting intermittently—if you hit the ball in between gusts, you'll airmail the green entirely. You need a shot that will fly close to 110 yards regardless of how hard the wind is blowing when you hit the shot. The knockdown 8-iron is the perfect choice.

The setup: First, play the ball back in your stance, to the right of center *(6-15)*. That will decrease the loft of the 8-iron so it doesn't balloon up into the wind. Set up open with your feet and shoulders aligned to the left. This is a control shot, so you don't need to make a big swing. The open stance will shorten your backswing *(6-16)* considerably and make it easier to clear your left hip on the downswing—another important requirement.

The swing: Follow the axiom, "When it's breezy, swing easy." You

6-17: *Through impact, let the toe of the club-head rotate so it is facing the sky. See how low the ball is flying? That's an 8-iron I'm using!*

don't want to make a fast, jerky swing. Swing rhythmically with an even tempo. On the downswing, think of clearing your left hip by turning it to the left. Accelerate through the ball, keeping your hands well forward. Keep your head down and hit down on the ball firmly. Let the clubhead rotate so the toe points at the sky on the follow-through (6-17).

C h a p t e r   7

W E D G E
W I Z A R D R Y

I'VE HOLED SHOTS FROM INSIDE 100 YARDS many times, but my most
memorable shot from close range wasn't quite that spectacular. It came
during the third round of the 1994 Memorial Tournament at Muirfield
Village Golf Club in Dublin, Ohio. The 11th hole there is a par 5 that's
too long for me to reach in two shots. I always lay up with my second so
I have optimum yardage for my approach, which for me is 90 to 95
yards. That approach is never easy due to the green. It slopes severely
from right to left, so after the ball lands it always coasts a considerable
distance to the left of where you've aimed.

The hole that day was cut on the left side of the green, which is
protected by a large bunker. I was in the middle of the fairway, 95 yards
from the hole. To go directly at the hole required a high wedge shot with
lots of spin—one of the hardest shots for me to play. I decided to get the
ball close via an unconventional route. I didn't want to flirt with that
bunker, so I aimed my 56-degree sand wedge at the right side of the
green and set up to play an intentional draw. I aligned my feet and
shoulders to the right and played the ball back in my stance so the ball
would fly low and release after it landed. The shot came off just as I
planned. It landed on the right side of the green, skipped once, caught

the slope and spun to the left. It rolled maybe 30 feet and stopped within three feet of the hole. I made the birdie putt.

I choose that incident as an example of shotmaking because it involved virtually all of the elements of a nonconventional shot: different ball position and alignment, different curvature and trajectory, specialized strategy to avoid that bunker on the left and an active imagination that enabled me to "see" an unusual path to the hole.

Professionals and top amateurs almost always try to hit the ball close to the hole from 100 yards and in. Even with the bunker in the way, my goal on the 11th hole at Muirfield was to hit the ball close enough to make a birdie. Weaker players merely try to hit the ball *somewhere on the green.* Therein lies one of the biggest obstacles to lowering your handicap. Of the total number of tee-to-green shots an average golfer hits during a round, at least one-third of them are from between 20 and 100 yards of the green. Most of your third shots on par-5 holes are from this distance. I see the 20- to 100-yard shot played on a lot of par-4 holes, too, due to poor tee shots, duffed second shots, or simply being a short hitter. In any case, this is where most shots are played. And it's the weakest part of the average player's game. Even modest improvement from this distance will automatically knock five strokes off your handicap.

The improvement I promise will come through better control of distance. Because hooks and slices aren't much of a factor in the wedge game (the high loft of the clubface reduces sidespin and curvature), your main goal is to hit the ball on line and make it fly within a couple of yards, long or short, of where you're aiming. Excellent distance control from 100 yards and in requires three things: (1) good technique, (2) increased feel and (3) sand wedges specifically designed for use from the fairway.

It may be that you can't carry the ball 100 yards with your sand wedge. No problem there; I use the expression "100 yards and in" subjectively anyway. Merely scale your personal range back depending on the maximum distance you hit your stronger sand wedge. I say "stronger" sand wedge because I suggest you carry *two* sand wedges. One sand wedge should have about 56 degrees of loft, useful for longer shots from the fairway. Your second sand wedge should have closer to 60 degrees of loft. It's useful from 60 yards and closer, and for around greens. To make room for two sand wedges in your set, take the 2-iron out of your bag. If you want to carry three fairway woods, which could help, take the 3-iron out as well.

FIND A SAND WEDGE
YOU CAN COUNT ON

I define the pitching wedge as a short iron and included it in the previous chapter because the pitching wedge is designed and plays just like the other short irons. It's merely a continuation of the standard set. There is very little weight distributed along the sole of the clubhead and its loft—usually in the 49-degree range—is merely a graduation downward from the other clubs. That's too little loft for shots played from within 100 yards. You'll hit the ball too low to make it stop quickly and the minimal amount of sole-weighting contributes to the difficulty of hitting the ball high.

For shots played from within 100 yards, you should go with the sand wedge *(7-1, right)*. The sand wedge is ideal because it has plenty of loft (anywhere from 55 to 60 degrees) and plenty of sole weighting, both of which help you hit the ball high. It's also a bit shorter than the standard pitching wedge and that allows more control. Finally, the sand wedge is more forgiving from bad lies because the leading edge tends to be rounded and penetrates through grass better.

Eye appeal, overall weight and plain personal preference are extremely important when choosing a sand wedge. But regardless of the style of sand wedge you use, the most important factor is the configuration of the sole. You don't want one with too much "bounce," the term used to describe how far the flange protrudes below the leading edge of the clubface. Although generous bounce helps you get the ball out of sand because it prevents the clubhead from digging into the sand, it isn't very conducive to shots from the fairway. If you hit behind the ball only a little, the clubhead will bounce off the turf and hit the ball thin. You want more forgiveness.

7-1: *The sand wedge on the left is a 60-degree model featuring a wide flange with plenty of "bounce" that's difficult to see in this photo. It's very useful from greenside bunkers. The sand wedge on the right, which I use on fairway shots of 70 to 100 yards, is a 56-degree model with minimal bounce.*

From inside roughly 60 yards, you should use a 60-degree wedge with plenty of bounce *(7-1, left)*. There are ways of playing the "hated half-wedge" shot with this club that don't bring the bounce of the club into play. And, as I'll explain in Chapters 9 and 10, you'll want plenty of bounce so you can negotiate the poor lies you get near the green, including those you experience in greenside bunkers.

'FEEL' FIRST, MECHANICS SECOND

It's very difficult to commit to memory a swing that will make the ball go exactly 70 yards every time. The line between a 70-yard swing and a 75-yard swing is just too fine to program mechanically. Hitting the ball 70 yards exactly requires the intangible element of feel, a sort of intuition that tells you how long your swing should be and how hard you should hit the ball. Feel for distance is acquired by seeing the distance to the hole and waiting for your brain to translate that distance into body motion. I've stated that amateurs lack the ability to play shots from 100 yards and closer. The main culprit is lack of feel.

To improve your feel for distance, you first need to become more familiar with the nuances of your sand wedge. Carry it around with you. Hold it. Waggle it. Practice swing it. Get used to its weight, the way it looks when you set it behind the ball at address. When you're watching television, hold your sand wedge lightly in your hands and extend it in front of you, acquiring a sense of how the clubhead feels in your hands. Try to make the clubhead weigh as much as it can by letting your hands go "dead." This kind of by-play with your sand wedge is extremely useful, especially when you go for long periods without playing.

Second, devote more of your practice time to the sand wedge. That may sound obvious, but it still amazes me how little amateurs practice shots from 100 yards and in. Because shots from that distance consume one-third of the total number of shots you hit from tee to green, you should practice them one-third of your practice time. When you practice, aim for a specific target. Try this drill, which I learned with Dr. Coop: After you hit the ball, keep your head down for an instant and assess whether you were long, short or right on the money with the shot. Then look up to see where the ball actually landed. Also, find out how far your maximum shot with the sand wedge flies. And remember, never try to make the ball go 10 yards farther than your full, comfortable swing allows. If you're outside that limit, go with the pitching wedge.

LET THE CLUB
DO THE WORK

One of the great killers of sand-wedge play is anxiety. On par-5 holes, there is anxiety and excitement over wanting to make a birdie. On par 4s, there is the grim concentration that results from trying to get up and down for a par. Either way, that extra charge of emotion leads to a habit that's as destructive as it is common: forcing the clubhead through the ball by overusing the hands.

By overusing the hands, I'm referring to the tendency of gripping the club too tightly and "forcing" the clubhead through the ball instead of letting it slide through of its own volition. I see too many players trying to help the ball into the air by hitting up on the ball or trying to make precise impact by gripping the club so tightly they look like they're going to twist the rubber grip right off the handle.

The hands lead the clubhead, but you have to trust that the clubhead will follow and get the ball airborne at impact with sufficient distance and plenty of spin. For that to happen, you have to hold the club lightly at address and throughout the swing. There is no need to force the clubhead into the ball. The clubhead will arrive at the ball in due time and in a square position that will start the ball right on line.

How do you know if you're overusing your hands? Examine the

7-2: If you can allow the clubhead to rotate naturally through impact so the toe is pointing at the sky on the follow-through, it's a sign you've let the club do the work.

position of the clubhead midway into the follow-through. If the toe of the club is pointing toward the sky (7-2), that means you've kept your hands soft and allowed the clubhead to rotate naturally. If the toe is pointing to the right of the target, your hands have been too tight, causing a blocking action through impact. Point that toe at the sky and you'll have much better feel and improved shot quality.

A SHORT SWING BEATS
AN EASY SWING

You may recall that with the short irons, I recommend a full but soft swing for those shots that require less than a full distance. My advice with the sand wedge is the dead opposite. If you face a 45-yard shot and

7-3, 7-4: On short, delicate shots with your sand wedge, it's best to shorten your backswing and then accelerate firmly through impact. You'll hit the ball more solidly this way and control distance better, too.

your optimal sand wedge range is 50 to 90 yards, don't try to ease off on the swing. Instead, shorten your backswing (7-3) and then accelerate the clubhead through the ball nice and firm (7-4). Trying to ease off a full swing will cause you to decelerate the clubhead through impact, which leads to poor distance control and fat and thin shots. Moreover, that soft swing doesn't produce nearly as much backspin. Instead, shorten your backswing by abbreviating your arm swing and body turn. Be deliberate on your backswing, so your body parts fire in correct sequence. Then swing aggressively through the ball.

That's one way to curtail distance. The other is to simply open the clubface at address. If you rotate the clubface open before you grip the club, you increase its loft. You can make a full swing and the ball will fly high but not as far. Don't worry about the ball squirting off to the right because with the sand wedge the ball tends to fly in the direction of the swing path, not in the direction the clubface is aimed.

To use that second technique, note that opening the clubface on most sand wedges also increases the bounce. That means less forgiveness on mis-hits. It's another factor to consider when buying a sand wedge—a sole that is ground so the bounce doesn't increase when you open the clubface.

KEEP LOWER BODY 'QUIET' THROUGHOUT SWING

The swing with the sand wedge is by definition shorter than with the other clubs. You don't need lots of leg and foot action because you're not trying for extra distance. Excessive lower body action reduces accuracy. It increases your range of motion at the expense of precise club-ball contact.

On the backswing, think of taking the club back with your arms and shoulders alone, leaving your hips, knees and feet out of the process. Your lower body will move, of course, but the idea is to retard its movement. Through impact, your legs should have a "dead" look and feel to them. Your right foot should be glued to the ground and your left leg should look the same as it did at address (7-5).

A good way to limit your hip turn is to imagine someone standing

7-5: Notice the passive appearance of my legs through impact. On short shots with your sand wedge, swing primarily with your upper body and keep your legs "quiet."

7-6: Your hips should turn slightly on sand wedge shots from the fairway, but note you can see both of my belt loops. For accuracy's sake, reduce your hip turn.

behind you at address, his hands placed on your hips. On the backswing, imagine he's trying to hold your hips in place so they don't rotate. They'll rotate some (7-6), but not enough to allow much movement in the feet and legs.

A second method is just as effective. At address, angle your right foot in toward the target so it is perpendicular to the target line. Normally, your right foot is turned out a fraction to allow the hips to turn. If you turn your right foot in, your hips can only turn a minimal amount before feeling resistance.

LET FOLLOW-THROUGH
DETERMINE DISTANCE

The length of your backswing determines the distance you hit the ball. But it's very difficult to regulate the length of your backswing when you're concentrating on hitting the ball solidly. The most efficient way to shorten your backswing is to shorten the length of your follow-through because one is a mirror-image of the other. If you face a shot where you don't need lots of distance, shortening your follow-through will guarantee that you accelerate the clubhead through impact, creating lots of spin.

HOW TO IMPART
FURIOUS BACKSPIN

One shot all top professionals have, and which eludes the average player, is the one where the ball takes one bounce, stops, then spins back toward the hole. Amateurs tend to view the shot almost as a magic trick, as though the pros know a secret they don't want to reveal. In fact, the answer is based purely on physics.

To make the ball stop quickly, you first have to position the ball back in your stance, slightly to the right of center. This insures that the clubhead will travel downward on a steep angle at impact and pinch the ball off the turf. The amateurs who hit wedge shots that have no "juice" on the ball simply don't apply the right type of swing. They position the ball too far forward and then scoop the ball off the turf. That shot has hardly any spin at all.

Imparting furious backspin requires more than just hitting down steeply into the back of the ball. For one thing, you have to keep your head rock-still on the downswing, so the clubhead can do its work. If you move your head forward, you'll disrupt not only your angle of approach with the clubhead but the speed at which the clubhead is moving. You want to trap the ball by keeping your hands forward of the clubhead through impact, not sliding your head and body forward. You want to feel your arms and hands passing your head on the downswing. Never let your head rise until well after the ball is gone (7-7).

The other key is conceptual. You want to visualize striking the ball

7-7: To impart lots of backspin, keep your head down through impact and don't let it slide toward the target. Don't look up until well after the ball is gone.

just below its equator. You might pretend the ball has little legs and that you're trying to chop them off. Or you might think of trying to shred the paint off the bottom portion of the ball. Either way, the key is to strike the ball cleanly and to avoid at all costs striking the turf behind the ball.

HOW TO HIT THE
'HATED HALF WEDGE'

No shot gives the everyday player fits like the delicate wedge shot from about 30 yards. The distance is too short to impart much spin on the ball, too long to play a bump-and-run to the green. No doubt about it, it's one of the toughest shots in the game—even for the best players.

7-8: The half-wedge shot is difficult even for better players, but you'll simplify it enormously by swinging the clubhead straight down the target line through impact, letting your right arm straighten. It should feel like you're throwing the clubhead straight at the target.

Your goal is to hit the ball high with lots of spin, and that's a tough combination. To hit the ball high you need to position the ball forward in your stance, and that makes it difficult to deliver a sharp downward blow. But it can be done, provided you practice the shot often and utilize a couple of special principles.

The first principle is to make the clubhead extend toward the target after impact. On normal shots the clubhead will swing to the left after impact. With the half-wedge shot, you want to make the clubhead travel well down the target line because that preserves clubface loft. You don't want the clubface to turn over on this shot because that reduces loft and causes the ball to come off too low.

To make the clubhead extend down the target line, straighten your right arm through impact (7-8). By the time the clubhead reaches knee-height on the follow-through, the clubshaft and your right arm should describe a straight, unbroken line. You want to feel like you're throwing the clubhead toward the target.

The second principle concerns your equipment. As I mentioned, you need a 60-degree wedge. There's only so much you can do with your swing to create loft with the clubface, and by choosing a 60-degree wedge the job is taken care of. But be careful: Your 60-degree wedge should have sufficient bounce along the sole to make it useful from around the greens, and that bounce can mean trouble on the half-wedge shot. You can't hit behind the ball. That's where practice comes in. When you practice this shot, make sure you're hitting the ball first by inspecting your divots. Your divots should begin slightly in front of the ball.

ATTACKING DIFFERENT
HOLE LOCATIONS

My philosophy of playing iron shots into greens is to aim for the middle of the green and curve the ball toward the hole. I recommend this strategy to every golfer regardless of skill level because it provides the biggest margin for error while preserving the opportunity to hit the ball close to the hole.

Let's say the hole is located on the right side of the green. If you aim for the center of the green and deliberately try to fade the ball toward the hole, you're rewarded with a great birdie opportunity if the shot comes off as planned. If, on the other hand, you fail to fade the ball and hit it dead straight, you'll be in the center of the green with a very good two-putt opportunity. This knowledge relaxes you psychologically and you'll make a much more aggressive, positive swing.

This strategy is much better than shooting straight at the flagstick. If the hole is cut on the right side of the green and you aim dead straight at the flagstick, you leave yourself open to all kinds of mistakes. A straight shot is the hardest shot in golf to hit, and if you fade the ball by accident, you'll miss the green to the right, leaving yourself a difficult pitch. Aiming straight at the flagstick is one of the biggest tactical mistakes you can make. Even if you're hitting the ball well and your shots are coming off perfect every time, you'll make too many bogeys aiming right at the hole.

If this strategy seems a bit conservative, so be it. I think of it as smart golf. Shooting good scores isn't just a matter of making birdies, it's avoiding bogeys. I'd much rather shoot a round of 68 that consisted of four birdies and 14 pars than a 68 comprised of six birdies, two bogeys and 10 pars. Good shotmaking doesn't just create scoring opportunities, it helps you avoid situations where you throw strokes away.

There are five basic hole locations on every green. Here is the shotmaking strategy you should adopt for each, presuming you have to land the ball on the green rather than play a run-up shot.

Back-right: You have lots of green to work with, so the smart shot here is to hit a low fade and let the ball land short of the hole and run to it. A low shot is a high-percentage shot because you're playing the ball back in your stance a bit and increasing your chances of solid contact. If you hit the ball straight, fine. You're in the middle of the green and have an easy two-putt. If the ball comes up a bit short of your target, that's OK, too, because you'll have an uphill putt—the easiest kind.

Back-left: This hole location asks for a low draw. You'll want to land the ball short of the flag in that wide-open portion of the green and let it roll back to the hole. It isn't wise to try to hit the ball high. A high shot tends to stop close to where it lands, and if you try to carry the ball all the way back to the hole and you're long, you'll have a difficult downhill chip shot. If you come up short, there's a chance you'll be very short and miss the green entirely. The low draw is the high-percentage play.

Front-right: When the flagstick is up front, you want to hit the ball high to a spot 10 feet past the hole. This hole location is made to order for a high fade. A low shot is no good unless the turf in front of the green is very firm. You want to insure that you get the ball on the green even if you're past the flagstick because a chip to a flagstick from short of the green can be one of the most difficult there is. So take plenty of club, move the ball up in your stance, and hit that high approach.

Front-left: You want to hit the ball high because the flagstick is up front, and you want to hit a draw that starts at the middle of the green. A high draw is one of the most difficult shots for the average player to hit, so aim for the center of the green and be satisfied with a two-putt for par.

Center of the green: Surprisingly, this is the most difficult pin to shoot at. Why? Because it doesn't tell you just by looking at it what type of shot to hit. Do you draw or fade the ball? High shot or low? The flagstick invites you to hit the ball right at it, but it puts the biggest demand on your creativity and patience.

The best rule of thumb is to go with your best natural shot. If you fade the ball, aim left of the hole and hit a fade. Don't give in to the temptation to try a shot you aren't gifted at hitting. And whatever you do, don't try to hit a shot straight at the flag. Try to curve the ball one way or the other. If you aim at the hole and draw or fade the shot, the ball will work away from the hole. If you aim away from the hole and play a curving shot you can depend on, the ball will work toward the hole—maybe too much, maybe not enough, but always getting closer.

Chapter 8

PITCHING
LIKE A PRO

To this point we've covered the full swing, which for the most part has entailed building a repeating motion rooted in sound fundamentals. My approach has largely been mechanical, the theory being that most golfers can develop a dependable long game through practice and intelligent application of certain full-swing principles. There's no doubt you can compensate for lack of raw talent and physical limitations through lots of practice. After all, Ed Furgol won the 1954 U.S. Open despite having a withered left arm. Billy Burke won the 1931 U.S. Open despite missing the ring and little fingers on his left hand. Bobby Cruickshank, who finished second in two U.S. Opens, stood only 5-foot-3. And like I said, I'm no giant.

But golf from 20 yards and in is an entirely different game. Technique is important, but intangible factors such as touch, feel and imagination play a dramatic role. Any touring pro will concede that a little heaven-sent talent in the areas of pitching, chipping and putting account for the difference in skill level between them and scratch-handicap amateurs. While fans are awed by the modern pro's driving and iron play, it's their magical skill from 20 yards and in that enables them to shave an extra three or four strokes from their scores almost every time they tee it up. That's the essential difference between pros and amateurs—three or four strokes a round.

I believe, however, that touch, feel, imagination and versatility can be learned. Maybe not to a degree that will make you an expert, due to the average player's time constraints and lack of experience. But improving your feel on shorter shots even a little will produce a sharp, noticeable improvement in your game. And if you combine improved feel with sound mechanics and a knowledge of playing a few specialty shots around the greens, your improvement will be dramatic. You'll save lots of pars, make a few birdies and develop the confidence necessary to elevate your game to a higher level.

One advantage of a more well-rounded pitching game is that you'll be a better player under pressure. Under the gun in tournaments, amateurs' adrenaline and nerves tend to work against them rather than in their favor. What touch they have deserts them completely and they fall apart. If you can develop trust in your feel, you'll perform much better when something is on the line.

To cite an example from my own experience, at the 1991 Bob Hope Chrysler Classic I wound up tied with Mark O'Meara after 90 holes. On the first hole of the sudden-death playoff, my second shot to the green came up eight yards short in the first cut of rough. Mark was already on the green in two, so I knew that I had to get the ball up and down to have a chance. The green was slightly elevated and the hole was cut 15 feet beyond the front of the green. That isn't much green to work with and I needed to hit a high pitch shot that landed softly.

I chose my 60-degree sand wedge and opened the clubface to increase its loft even more. I placed my feet close together and gripped the club very lightly. Although I was very nervous, by holding the club lightly I was acutely aware of its weight and immediately gained a sense of how hard to hit the ball. I made a short, three-quarter backswing and on the downswing cut across the ball from outside-to-inside. I just let the clubhead slide under the ball. It popped high into the air, landed on the green about 10 feet short of the hole, rolled forward and dropped into the center of the cup. Mark missed his putt to tie, and my son,

Ryan (who was 6 at the time), charged onto the green, faking one of the marshals out of his shoes to get to me. The shot I made to win was exciting, but watching Ryan run up to me was more memorable!

Feel, combined with good mechanics, enabled me to hole the shot. In this chapter I'll discuss several ways to improve your touch and feel on pitches and how to apply it to the different situations you'll face around the greens.

FEEL CLUB IN THE 'TRIGGER' FINGER
OF YOUR RIGHT HAND

The chief way that a pitch shot differs from a chip shot is that the pitch requires a fair amount of wrist break in the swing. Many pitches require a high ball flight and plenty of carry, even though you're not hitting the ball very far. So you need to apply some clubhead speed and that requires hand and wrist action. You're not just tapping the ball, you're striking the ball with some force.

The first priority is to hold the club lightly. Because you're hitting the ball to a precise spot on the green, there's a tendency to grip the club tightly and force the club onto the ball. But holding the club this way causes the reverse to happen. You'll swing the club in a fast, jerky manner. You'll swing the club along a faulty path. You won't hit the ball solidly. A light grip pressure makes it possible to "throw" the ball onto the green with sensitivity and a feel for distance.

Take your sand wedge and hold it horizontally in front of you, just firmly enough to keep the clubhead from falling to the ground. Open your hands slightly and heft the club, trying to make it feel heavy in your hands. Get a sense for the weight of the clubhead at the end of the shaft. You should feel the club pressing down on the index finger of your right hand, which is extended slightly as though you were ready to pull the trigger on a gun. Now make a series of small, rhythmic practice swings, maintaining that sense of softness in your hands. Brush the top of the grass lazily, swinging the club back and through without interruption. You should eventually be able to do it with your eyes closed.

This is the type of sensation you want to have when playing any pitch shot. At first, you'll probably find that your grip pressure increases when you actually hit balls. But your goal should be to grip the club as lightly as when you're performing the practice drill.

STANDARD SETUP:
ALIGN EVERYTHING OPEN

My philosophy on standard pitches is to hit the ball high enough to allow it to land softly and roll a very short distance. I use my sand wedges on almost all basic pitch shots because they have more loft than my other clubs. But to insure maximum loft I align my feet, hips and shoulders open at address, well left of my target *(8-1)*.

8-1: On standard pitch shots, aim the clubface at your target but align your feet, hips and shoulders dramatically to the left. This will help you maintain the loft of your sand wedge through impact.

The open setup promotes an outside-to-inside swing in relation to the target, much like a standard full-swing shot where I'm trying to fade the ball. This makes my angle of approach steeper, so very little grass will intervene between the ball and clubface. By setting up open, I also effectively increase clubface loft, and that means a higher, softer shot.

I should point out that on pitch shots the ball will not fade despite the outside-to-inside swing you'll make. That's because you're not hitting the ball hard enough to impart sufficient sidespin to make the ball curve. Moreover, on the pitching swing the ball will start out where the clubface is aimed—right at your target—rather than where your body is aligned. This is an important departure from the standard full-swing shot, where the ball starts out where your body is aligned and then curves toward the direction you aimed the clubface.

GRIP PROCEDURE
IS CRITICAL

When you align your body to the left of the target at address but aim the clubface directly *at* the target, you want to guarantee that those conditions are preserved at impact. The lion's share of that job falls to your grip—or rather, the procedure of placing your hands on the club correctly. On all pitch shots, aim the clubface at the target first, the handle resting lightly in your hands (8-2). Don't close your fingers on the handle just yet. Only after everything is in place—your body alignment and clubface position—should you close your hands on the club (8-3). Now there is no way you'll close the clubface at impact, which would hit the ball low and hot instead of high and soft.

TWO WAYS TO
CONTROL DISTANCE

Distance control is critical in pitching. One of the benefits of light grip pressure is increased sensitivity in your hands, which in turn provides the intuitive sense for how far the ball will fly on a given pitch. But there are two mechanical adjustments that will enhance distance con-

8-2, 8-3: *One of the worst things you can do on pitch shots is close the clubface through impact. The key to preventing this is your gripping procedure. Always aim the clubface at the target first (left), then complete your grip.*

trol and, combined with a sense of feel, will result in pinpoint precision.

The first is the degree to which you open the clubface at address. The farther you open the clubface, the higher the ball will fly and the shorter the distance it will travel forward. On virtually all pitch shots you should open the clubface some because you want the ball to fly high enough to prevent it from rolling too far after it lands. One of the benefits of choosing a 56-degree sand wedge without a lot of bounce (see Chapter 7) is that you can open the clubface a lot without causing the leading edge to extend too far above the ground. How far you should open the clubface for a particular shot can only be determined by experimenting. It's more an art than it is a science.

The second method for controlling distance is to vary the length of your follow-through. As I explained in Chapter 7, thinking of making a short follow-through will produce a short shot because it has the effect of shortening your backswing. If anything, this technique is even more important on pitch shots. Trying to regulate the length of your backswing is very difficult, but shortening (or lengthening) your follow-through is simple and will control the distance your pitch shot flies.

HEAD DOWN THROUGH IMPACT— AND BEYOND

Also vital to distance control is solid club-ball contact. No matter how soft you keep your hands or how well you adhere to good swing mechanics, if you hit the ball on the heel or toe of the club, your pitch will come up short. The only way to achieve solid contact consistently is to keep your head down through impact. Thinking "head down" also helps you shake off the anxiety of wanting to know where the ball went after you hit it. Anxiety, you know, is a killer on pitch shots. It causes you to think of how badly you want to hit a good pitch, rather than of the feel and swing mechanics that will *produce* a good pitch.

When you swing the club down and through impact (8-4 *through* 8-6), keep your eyes riveted on the ball. Think only of how hard you want to hit the shot. Keep your head down until the ball is well on its way to the target and your follow-through is almost complete. Not only will this help you hit the ball solidly, it will help you deliver the necessary downward blow through impact.

KEEP KNEES
CLOSE TOGETHER

Because you're not making a long swing, you don't need much lower body motion. Adding excess movement in your hips, legs and feet just creates more opportunity for mistakes. You want to keep your legs as still as possible and a good way to do that is to place your feet fairly

8-4—8-6: Keys to better pitching: Keep your head down at all times, your eyes riveted on the ball, and keep your knees close together during the swing.

close together at address (8-4). By keeping your feet close together, you reduce unnecessary hip rotation and weight shifting during the swing.

To further restrict motion in your feet, legs and hips, keep your knees together throughout the swing. Flex them slightly at address so they feel lively, but don't let them separate on the backswing (8-5) or on the follow-through (8-6). Pretend your legs are in a cast, and perform the swing with your shoulders, arms and hands only. This will increase your chances for solid contact and put the onus on your upper body, where it belongs.

With your feet and knees close together, you don't have a very wide

foundation for maintaining your balance. But to insure that you stay "centered" throughout the swing, make sure you swing rhythmically with good tempo. There's no hurry. The backswing should be leisurely, and the downswing should occur at the same even pace with no sudden acceleration of the hands and arms. Any increase in speed on the downswing should be produced gradually, maxing out through impact. And I emphasize that the clubhead should be *gaining* speed through impact, not losing speed. Never decelerate.

STRATEGY: AIM FOR
A THREE-FOOT CIRCLE

The different lies you get, the elevation and firmness of the green, the hole location and slope of the green, are all factors that demand you "see" the shot in your mind's eye before you hit it. As you evaluate your lie and the type of shot you want to hit, picture the ball flying in the air on a trajectory that will allow the ball to land with the softness and roll necessary to allow it to cozy up to the hole.

When you picture the ball landing on the green, envision a circle where you want the ball to touch down. The circle is an intermediate target and if you can make the ball land within it, your chances of getting the ball close are greater than if you focus on the hole itself. At first you may want to aim for a circle about six feet in diameter. Gradually, however, you should narrow that circle down to about three feet. If the circle is too big, you won't concentrate sharply enough to hit the ball precisely. If the imaginary circle is smaller, you'll get too precise and allow tension to creep in. Three feet is about right.

SOFT LOB OVER
A BUNKER

The short pitch to a flagstick placed just over a greenside bunker is one of the most nerve-racking in the game. There's only one option: a high ball flight with plenty of backspin. It's a tough shot because you need to hit the ball firmly without making a long swing. This shot, more than any other, breeds the disastrous mistakes of trying to help the ball into the air and lifting your head before impact. Your biggest enemies are anticipation and anxiety.

Build in as much margin for error as you can with your setup and type of swing you make. Start by placing the ball in the center of your stance, maybe even a bit to the right of center (8-7). Don't place it farther forward than that in an effort to hit the ball higher because it's just too difficult to deliver the necessary descending blow. You'll be tempted to try to scoop the ball into the air. Play the ball in the center of your stance and obtain the high ball flight by using your 60-degree sand

8-7: Although the soft lob over a bunker requires height on the shot, you still should play the ball to the right of center in your stance at address. This makes it easier to obtain precise club-ball contact.

8-8: *Although I positioned the ball back in my stance, note I haven't taken a divot. The idea is to slide the clubhead under the ball. Don't hammer down into the ball or it will come out too low and hot.*

wedge. Open your stance as well to promote an outside-to-inside swing path in relation to your body. That encourages a steeper angle of approach and decreases the odds of hitting the ball thin.

Keep your hands and arms relaxed and focus on a positive result. Take the club back slowly and smoothly. You don't need a long backswing, but you don't consciously want to cut the backswing short, either. The change of direction from the top should be smooth, flowing and unhurried.

8-9: To maintain club-face loft, don't let the clubhead rotate through impact and into the follow-through. Note that both the clubface and my right palm are facing upward. That's a good goal for your follow-through.

On the forward swing, don't think of chopping down steeply on the back of the ball. Merely try to slide the clubhead underneath the ball, taking a very small divot, if any (8-8). Because you need to hit the ball high, don't close the clubface. Keep it open even after the ball is gone (8-9). Think of the clubface as being an extension of your right hand. If your right hand rotates to a palm-down position, the clubface will close as well. Keep your right palm facing the sky on the follow-through and you'll keep the clubface open.

8-10: To make the ball fly high and soft, you want to emulate throwing the ball under-handed toward the target.

The action on the downswing can also be likened to throwing a ball underhand with your right hand (8-10). Instead of throwing a ball, however, you're throwing the clubhead. Just make sure the clubhead doesn't pass your hands until well after impact.

PITCH TO A
TWO-TIERED GREEN

Some greens are constructed on two levels, the front half usually lower than the back half. The front portion of the green is usually fairly flat but then rises abruptly to the upper tier. When the flagstick is on the upper tier, you have a dilemma: Do you fly the ball all the way to the back of the green, or should you try to land the ball on the front half and let it run back to the hole?

There's a downside to each shot. If you try to fly the ball onto the second tier but come up a little short, the ball will roll down the hill and you'll be left with a very difficult two-putt. If you play a low run-up shot but don't hit the ball hard enough, the same thing will happen. And if you hit the ball too firmly, you'll have a tough downhill putt that will roll to the front of the green.

In almost all cases, I believe the run-up shot is the better choice. You have more control because the ball spends more time on the ground than in the air. There also is more margin for error because you don't need to make as long a swing.

The procedure starts with club selection. Go with an 8- or 9-iron rather than the sand wedge because you want to hit the ball low without making radical adjustments in your setup and ball position. Next, use a putting grip with your hands turned away from each other to restrict wrist movement. You don't need much wrist break on this shot.

On the backswing extend the clubhead directly down the target line. Don't take the club back outside because you'll have to cut across the ball through impact and that produces a higher ball flight. As you swing through, think of sticking the clubhead into the ground just after you strike the ball. That will insure a downward blow. The ball will come out low without too much backspin, which is good because you don't want the ball to check up. You want it to release and roll as if you were tossing it with your hand.

Strategy on the run-up shot is critical. At all costs, you must get the ball on the second tier. If you get it on the upper tier, you very well might one-putt—two-putt at worst. If you leave it on the lower tier, however, you bring a three-putt into the equation. You want to avoid that worst-case scenario.

PITCHING FROM
SIDEHILL LIES

The most dramatic contouring on a hole occurs within 20 yards of the green. Bunkers, dips, swales, mounds and sideslopes result in a lot of pitches played from sidehill lies with the ball above or below your feet. These are specialty shots that require dramatic changes in your setup and swing.

- *Ball above your feet:* First and foremost, never alter your normal posture. You don't want to stand taller by raising your back or removing the flex from your knees. Posture changes throw your pitching swing out of kilter. Adjust by choking down on the handle until the clubhead is seated naturally behind the ball *(8-11)*.

  Second, aim well to the right of your target. When the ball is above your feet, at address the clubshaft is much flatter or closer to parallel with the horizon. That changes the clubface angle so it effectively is aimed to the left of your target. The tendency is to pull the shot to the left, so compensate by aiming to the right.

  Finally, hold on firmly with your left hand through impact. The sideslope will cause you to make a sweeping action with the clubhead through impact *(8-12)* rather than a descending action, and that brings the grass behind the ball into play. Hold on firmly with your left hand and the grass won't twist the clubface closed through the hitting area.

- *Ball below your feet:* The problem is to try to reach the ball, and because your sand wedge is only so long, you have to compensate by adjusting your posture. Do this by increasing the flex of your knees *(8-13)* rather than stooping over more at the waist. This swing is performed with the upper body, so you want to preserve your normal back posture as much as possible. You should also aim to the left of the hole because the sidehill will tend to make the ball pop out to the right of where you're aiming.

  It's difficult to hit the ball high when the ball is below you, so you need to make the type of swing that will encourage a high trajectory. Take the club back outside so your hands won't collide

8-11, 8-12: When the ball is above your feet, you should adjust by standing tall at address, choking down on the club and aiming to the right of the target (top). Through impact (left), hold on firmly with your left hand and deliver a sweeping-type blow, sliding the clubhead under the ball.

8-13, 8-14: When the ball is below your feet, adjust by increasing the flex in your knees at address and aim left of your target. Through impact, keep your head still and think only of making clean contact.

with your right knee. On the downswing, cut across the ball from outside-to-inside. Maintain the position of your back *(8-14)*, keep your head still and try to clip the ball cleanly.

THE DIFFICULT
DOWNHILL PITCH

You've hit the ball over the green, you've got a downhill lie and the flag-stick is in the back of the green. You don't have much green to work with. Worse, the ball is on a downslope, which promotes a low-flying shot. How do you hit the ball high so it lands softly? It's a very demanding shot. Start by widening your stance to restrict leg movement. Widening your stance tends to lower your upper body toward the ground, so you need to compensate by choking down on the club. Play the ball back in your stance because playing it forward of center will cause you to overextend your arms in order to make the clubhead reach the ball.

Next, open the clubface—a lot. You need all the loft you can create because of the downslope. Now make a fairly long swing (8-15), taking the club back on an outside path. The long swing shouldn't cause you to hit the ball too far because the loft you've added to the clubface by opening it, combined with choking down on the club, will take distance off the shot. On the downswing, make the clubhead travel parallel with the downslope through impact, so the ball pops softly into the air (8-16). You shouldn't try to hit down sharply on the ball, nor should you try to help it into the air by scooping it. Maintain the loft of the clubface by keeping it open and the ball will pop into the air. *Maintain your knee flex well into the follow-through (8-17).*

The shot will come out with very little backspin but will land in a "dead" manner. Aim for a spot well short of the hole, so the slope will take over and trickle the ball down to the cup.

NEAT SHOT: BALL SUSPENDED
IN TALL GRASS

Even the best player dreads finding his ball sitting down in tall grass. Ironically, the shorter the shot from tall grass, the harder it is to play. You need to generate enough clubhead speed to make the clubhead penetrate the grass, but not so much that you hit the ball over the green if

151

8-15—8-17: The downhill pitch. After opening the clubface at address, make a fairly long backswing. Through impact, make the clubhead travel level with the slope so the ball pops up abruptly. On the follow-through, maintain the flex in your knees.

you happen to strike the ball too cleanly. The grass makes this one of the most unpredictable shots in the game. The only way to play the shot is as if it were buried in sand, hitting behind the ball with a ferocious, outside-to-inside swing, the clubface set wide open.

Then there is the case where the ball is in tall grass but hasn't fallen all the way down to the ground. The ball is suspended about midway down to the ground, so there's plenty of space between the ball and the turf *(8-18)*. If you play the shot as though the ball were sitting down, the clubhead may slide under the ball completely, hardly touching it. If

you try to chip it cleanly, the tall grass will grab the clubhead and kill its momentum.

This is one of the oddest shots you'll encounter around the greens and it takes an unusual method to play it well. First, play the ball to the right of center in your stance, so you'll deliver a descending blow and hit the ball crisply. Second, choke down on your sand wedge the same amount that the ball is suspended above the ground. Inspect your lie closely to ascertain just how far above the ground the ball is suspended. At address, don't ground the club—you may cause the ball to move, for

8-18: Sometimes your ball comes to rest suspended midway between the top of the grass and the ground below. The tendency is to undercut the ball so severely that you barely strike it at all.

8-19: The solution is to position the ball back in your stance and aim the leading edge of the clubface at the base of the ball. That insures clean club-ball contact and a predictable result.

154

which you'll incur a one-stroke penalty. Just aim the leading edge of the clubface at the base of the ball (8-19), which is precisely where you want to make contact.

The pitching swing you make is dictated by your setup. Swing naturally and the clubhead will be moving downward when you strike the ball, due to your playing the ball back in your stance. The ball will pop up in the air abruptly and land very softly, without much backspin.

Chapter 9

CHIPPING WITH
PRECISION

I'VE ALWAYS VIEWED CHIPPING as one of the more dynamic parts of the game. An effective chipping game requires more creativity and versatility than you may think. Most of the elements that go into the full swing—club selection, ball position, programming a swing to fit the shot—are present in chipping as well. There are so many aspects of chipping, I never find it boring. In fact, it's one of the parts of the game I enjoy practicing the most.

Chipping is one of the areas of the game that matters most, but among amateurs it certainly is the part that is practiced the least. Walk onto any practice area in America and you'll always find more players beating balls on the range than practicing their chipping. Most golfers view chipping as unrewarding drudgery. In fact, poor chipping is a primary reason the handicap of the average golfer has remained frozen at 18 for the last 25 years.

Chipping is critical for the simple reason that even expert golfers miss several greens per round with their iron shots. The only way to score well is to consistently chip the ball so close to the hole that you can't help but make your share of par-saving putts. Poor chippers invariably attribute their high scores to their poor driving or putting, all the while ignoring the fact that their sloppy short game is the true reason they shot a high score.

The time I spend practicing pays off heavily in several ways. The ability to get the ball up and down from all sorts of places around the green is demoralizing to opponents, especially long hitters who think they can manhandle players who are less skilled from tee to green.

When you feel like you can get the ball into the hole with a chip and one putt, it fills you with confidence and instills a healthy aggressiveness in your long game. You'll swing away much more freely when you know you can miss the green and still be confident of making par. You'll be a better, more versatile ball-striker as a result.

Chipping is so multidimensional that I've always considered it a game within a game. There are so many options to playing the standard chip shot. My best personal example came at the 1995 Ryder Cup Matches at Oak Hill Country Club in Rochester, N.Y., when I partnered with Loren Roberts in our Saturday four-ball match against Nick Faldo and Bernhard Langer. The match was all square as we played the 18th hole, a long, difficult par 4. My drive strayed into the rough and from there I hit a very good 4-iron shot that settled onto the back fringe about 20 feet from the hole. Loren hit the green in two, and when it was our turn to play we decided that Loren should putt first. He hit a very good putt and secured our par. Faldo was slightly farther from the hole than I was, but I played next.

There were several ways I could have played the shot. The chip was downhill and broke from right to left, and I could have used an 8-iron or even my putter to hit the ball close to the hole. The slope was so severe I even considered using my 60-degree sand wedge to make the ball pop high in the air and land softly. But because Loren already had his par, I wanted to be more aggressive, so I chose my pitching wedge.

I lined the shot up as though it were a putt, thinking more of the line than the speed. I moved the ball back in my stance to help me hit down on the ball solidly. I aimed about two feet to the right of the cup, knowing the ball would swing to the left after it started rolling. My last thought was of how hard to hit the ball. I wanted it to land just onto the green so it would spend more time on the ground than in the air.

The chip felt good the second I hit it. A bit strong maybe, but right on line with a true roll. It hit the back of the hole and went in. Nick missed his putt and we won the match. We lost the Ryder Cup the next day, but the excitement of holing that chip will stay with me forever.

I use one of three methods in chipping. Like I said, there are a lot of options in chipping. The style you employ determines how the ball behaves after it lands on the green. I'll describe each method in detail and explain some other principles of chipping that will improve your short game dramatically.

METHOD NO. 1:
CHIP LIKE YOU PUTT

When you are within five yards of the putting surface and there's plenty of green between your ball and the hole, you want the ball to cover most of that distance on the ground instead of in the air. You don't want to

9-1: The basic chipping grip, designed to restrict wrist movement. Your hands should be turned away from each other an equal amount on the handle.

impart backspin, as that makes judging the speed all the more difficult. Nor do you want to hit the ball high, as that also makes it difficult to hit the ball the right distance. Basically you want to hit your chip the way you would a putt and that means going to a less-lofted club, anything from a 6-iron to an 8-iron depending on what's more comfortable for you. I'm using an 8-iron in the accompanying photos.

This chip is performed with your putting grip. Position your hands on the club as though for a full swing, then rotate your hands in opposite directions so they're turned away from each other (9-1). Each hand should be turned the same amount.

Position the ball in the center of your stance. If you have difficulty chipping solidly, try playing the ball slightly to the right of center (9-2).

9-2—9-4: On basic chips, the triangle formed by your shoulders and arms should remain intact throughout the stroke. This simplifies the stroke and promotes solid contact.

Your hands should be directly above the ball. Your stance should be slightly open.

The putting grip restricts hand and wrist action. That's the idea with this shot; you want to perform the stroke with your arms and shoulders only. Imagine that your arms and shoulders form a triangle. You don't want to change the shape of the triangle on your backswing (9-3). Merely slide the clubhead under the ball through impact (9-4) and try to match the size of your follow-through with your backswing. Making them the same size promotes consistency and helps you control distance.

This is the method I used on that shot at the Ryder Cup. Although that shot wasn't a long one, my primary goal was to hit the ball on the correct line.

*9-5—9-7: When playing the "stab,"
use your normal full-swing grip to
promote hinging of the wrists on the
backswing. Keep your hands ahead
of the clubhead through impact and
complete the stroke immediately
after the clubhead strikes the ball.*

METHOD NO. 2:
THE STAB

Basically there are two ways to chip the ball low so it runs after landing.
In using Method No. 1, you get a low ball flight by choosing a less-lofted club. But chipping with a 6-, 7- or 8-iron isn't always feasible, especially if you're in light rough. Because you're playing the shot basically
the same way you stroke a putt, your angle of approach with the clubhead is very shallow and therefore can get tangled in the grass before
impact. That will ruin the shot.

The "stab" is an attractive alternative to Method No. 1 because it
can be used from all sorts of lies, even bad ones where the ball is sitting
down in light rough. Using a lofted club (your sand wedge, usually,

although you might also use a pitching wedge if your lie is good), start by using your regular full-swing grip and placing the ball well back in your stance, almost off your right foot (9-5). Let your wrists break a little on the backswing (9-6).

The key is the forward swing. Rather than let the club swing into the ball on its own, make sure your hands swing forward so they remain well ahead of the clubhead. At impact, let the clubhead finish about an inch ahead of the ball (9-7). Because you positioned the ball well back in your stance, you're forcing the clubhead into the ball on a very steep angle. The leading edge of the clubface should collide with the turf immediately after it strikes the ball. For a solid hit, keep your head down even after the clubhead has stopped.

The ball will come out low and run after it lands, much like it behaved in Method No. 1. The difference is that because the clubhead is approaching the ball on such a steep angle, the grass behind the ball won't interfere. It's a handy shot. You don't have to worry about the ball spinning because you've delofted the clubface by playing the ball back and keeping your hands ahead on the forward swing.

METHOD NO. 3:
THE MINI-LOB

This method is best for short shots when your ball is in light rough or you otherwise need extra help in making solid club-ball contact. It is not a good shot for longer chips because your stance, clubface position and swing are designed to produce a high ball flight. It's a very good method when you have to carry your ball over a larger amount of fringe, or you need to carry a small rise to reach the green. The ball lands softly, though not with much backspin because you aren't hitting the ball very hard.

Using your sand wedge, begin by using your normal full-swing grip because there is some wrist action involved in this shot. Open your stance and your shoulders as well. Take the club back slightly to the outside, letting your wrists break naturally (9-8). The downswing is performed like a miniature cut shot. Keep your hands soft so the clubhead almost falls onto the back of the ball and let the club travel along the line established by your stance. The outside-to-inside swing path, combined with the loft of your sand wedge, will cause the ball to pop high into the air for such a short shot (9-9). Don't look up until the ball is gone. Expect the ball to behave almost like a knuckleball, with very little spin and only as much roll as its forward speed permits.

A TRUE ROLL
IS CRUCIAL

You'll have more success trying to roll the ball most of the distance to the hole rather than trying to fly the ball to the hole. A low, running shot

9-8, 9-9: To play the "mini-lob," use your sand wedge and open your stance. Take the clubhead back to the outside and cut across the ball through impact. The loft and outside-to-inside swing path will produce a high, soft shot.

is more dependable and easier to control. You don't need to make as big a swing, therefore it's easier to hit the ball flush every time.

After you commit to this strategy, the next step is to impart as true a roll on the ball as possible. The next time you play with your high-handicap friends, look closely at the ball just as it comes off the club-face. I'm betting it doesn't come off with perfect end-over-end spin. If the ball is spinning sideways, it will bounce to one side of the line or the other when it strikes the green. All of your planning is wasted because the ball won't roll the way you intended it to.

The only way to impart a true roll is to take the clubhead straight back on the takeaway and swing straight through to the target after impact. A simple drill will help you perfect this. Place a tee about a foot behind the ball and down the target line at address and try to clip it with the clubhead on your backswing. On the forward swing, make the club-face travel directly down the line you want the ball to travel for a foot or so after impact. Watch the way the ball spins just after impact.

ACCELERATE
ON ALL CHIPS

Even though you're making a tiny swing, it's important to strike the ball assertively, with the clubhead gaining speed at the moment of impact. A decelerating swing is the No. 1 problem I see among amateurs who chip poorly. If the clubhead is losing speed as it approaches the ball, the flow of movement in your hands and arms will break down and you'll be in a very poor position at impact. All kinds of botched shots can result.

A chief cause of decelerating is sensing in midswing that you're going to hit the ball too far. The cure is simple. As you prepare to play the shot, make a couple of practice swings and concentrate on the force you intend to apply. If it seems like you may hit the ball too far, switch to a more lofted club. If the chip you're playing is very short and you've already chosen your sand wedge, try opening the clubface a bit. Adding loft will enable you to strike the ball more firmly without hitting it as far.

A DRILL FOR
QUICK ELEVATION

The principles for the full swing remain intact for chipping. You want to hit down on the ball to make the ball go up. If you try to help the ball into the air by scooping it, you'll hit the shot fat or thin. An effective way to train yourself to hit down on the ball is to place your golf bag five feet in front of you and practice chipping over it *(9-10)*. Use your 56-degree sand wedge and concentrate on hitting down directly into the back of the ball, keeping your head still and your legs and feet quiet. You'll find

9-10: *Controlling trajectory is as important in chipping as in the full swing. Chipping over obstacles during practice will train you to hit down on the ball rather than trying to scoop it into the air.*

that hitting down on the ball will make it pop into the air immediately, while scooping it causes it to come out lower.

DON'T CHOKE
DOWN ON CLUB

Chipping demands a lot of feel and great control of the club. Choking down on the club effectively makes the club lighter and makes it easier to maneuver the clubhead. But I believe in gripping your sand wedge about the same as you would for a standard full-swing shot. When you choke down, you're forced to change your posture to accommodate your

167

hands resting lower on the handle. Changing your posture is a dramatic adjustment that can alter the natural chipping motion.

If you feel it's necessary to choke down, don't go down more than half an inch or so. If you sense you don't have control of the club or that it feels heavy, slow down your swinging motion.

ENVISION A
TWO-LANE HIGHWAY

Although I believe in selecting the route the ball will travel to the hole when planning the chip, you should not try to picture a precise, razor-

9-11: When envisioning the ball's path to the hole, don't be too precise. Seeing in your mind's eye a broader path (I like to picture a two-lane highway) reduces stress and anxiety.

thin line you want the ball to follow. It's too stressful and unrealistic. If you picture that thin line and feel you *must* make the ball follow it at all costs, anxiety creeps in. You want to feel relaxed mentally as well as physically when chipping.

You'll have much better luck envisioning a broader path. I like to think of the path to the hole as a small two-lane highway *(9-11)*. Instill that image in your mind and trust your feel and mechanics to get the ball on track. You'll be amazed at how accurately your mind will send the right messages to your hands and arms.

The idea is not to hole every chip shot, so don't even try to be that precise. Get the ball rolling on that highway (going the speed limit, of course) and you'll hole your share.

SPEED CONTROL:
BE CONSERVATIVE

Had that chip shot for birdie at the '95 Ryder Cup Matches not gone in the hole, it would have rolled at least 10 feet past the hole. The chip obviously was going slowly enough to fall into the hole, but I did hit it very firmly because Loren was already assured of making par. Normally I would have hit the chip much softer. I believe in being cautious on all chips except when you absolutely have to hole it or when your partner in a four-ball match is already safely in the hole.

Try to chip the ball so it reaches the hole with just enough speed to topple over the front edge. Your main objective is to get up and down. If you're too aggressive, you'll have too many wicked comeback putts and nobody can hole all of those. Don't feel badly if your chip comes up a foot or two short of the hole. It's better than being four feet past.

UPHILL AND
DOWNHILL CHIPS

Not all your chipping lies are level, and the methods for playing uphill and downhill are drastically different. On uphill lies, set your upper body vertical, select a club with less loft and play the ball back in your

9-12: When chipping uphill, set your body vertical in relation to the horizon and play the ball back in your stance.

stance *(9-12)*. Your shoulders should be level with the horizon. The uphill lie will naturally make the ball come out higher, and you don't want to do anything with your club selection or setup to exaggerate that effect. The backswing is normal, but on the forward swing force the clubhead directly into the upslope so it finishes immediately after impact. This insures cleaner contact.

The downhill lie is trickier. You need to get the ball airborne more quickly because the downslope will naturally make the ball come out lower and you need enough carry to get the ball past the fringe. Set up with your weight on your downhill foot, your shoulders positioned parallel with the slope. Choose a club with plenty of loft, possibly your 60-degree sand wedge. Open the clubface to increase the loft even more. Play the ball farther forward in your stance than you would for an uphill lie. That way, you can reach the ball without straining *(9-13)*.

9-13: For the downhill chip, use the most lofted club in your bag and play the ball forward in your stance. Through impact, the club should travel parallel with the downslope.

On the downswing, make the club travel level with the downslope. It will be moving downward quite severely in relation to the horizon, but you need the steep angle of approach to make the clubhead slide under the ball. Make sure you accelerate. The ball will come out high and hard enough to carry the fringe.

FLAGSTICK IN
OR OUT?

There's always been a debate on chip shots as to whether it's best to leave the flagstick in the hole or to take it out. In truth, there are so many factors at work and skill levels vary so much that it's hard to dispense hard and firm advice for everyone. Generally, though, you'll have good success following one rule: On uphill chips take the flagstick out and on downhill chips leave it in.

Chipping uphill, you're striking the ball a bit more firmly, but the ball is dying faster and has a good chance of dropping without the flagstick acting as a backstop. Also, the hole is canted toward you a bit relative to the horizon, so the back of the hole itself acts as a backstop.

Downhill chips are another matter. The ball will maintain its speed and the hole is tilted away from you. Without the flagstick there to stop the ball, it must hit the hole dead center to drop. So the flagstick will help more often than not and should be left in *(9-14)*.

Inspect the hole on all short chips where holing the shot seems

9-14: On downhill chips, leaving the flagstick in the hole increases the chances of the ball dropping.

like a real possibility. If the flagstick is not centered in the hole, *take it out*. If the flagstick is leaning toward you, there may not be room to accommodate the ball and the rules state that all of the ball must be at rest below the surface before it is considered holed. If the flagstick is leaning to either side, that's bad, too.

There's one more argument for leaving the flagstick out on simple chips you think you can hole. Psychologically, it always helps my touch when I remove the flagstick from the hole. Invariably I chip the ball closer to the hole, probably because I know the flagstick isn't there to act as a backstop.

TWO NEAT SHOTS

1. Ball against fringe

Sometimes your ball will come to rest on the fringe of the green directly against the cut of rough. It's a perplexing shot for most amateurs because you know that if you play the chip conventionally, the clubhead will become snared in the tall grass just before impact. Putting the ball is out of the question for the same reason.

An effective (and easy) way to play the shot is to take your sand wedge and play the ball just forward of center in your stance. Aim the leading edge of the clubface at the ball's equator (*9-15*). Take the clubhead back steeply enough for it to clear the top of the grass. On the downswing deliver a descending blow so that the leading edge of the clubface strikes the ball's equator. Don't worry about driving the ball into the turf with the downward blow. The ball won't behave that way. It will skitter through the grass and actually become airborne (*9-16*). From there it will roll onto the green and track smoothly to the hole.

2. Chip with your putter

At the Million Dollar Challenge in Sun City, South Africa, the course features a particular variety of grass that is extremely tough and wiry. Around the greens, this grass is extremely difficult to chip from because striking behind the ball only a fraction results in the grass grabbing the

9-15, 9-16: When your ball rests on the edge of the fringe, use your sand wedge and aim the leading edge of the clubface at the ball's equator. Deliver a descending blow into the middle of the ball, and it will become airborne long enough to clear the fringe.

clubface and ruining the shot. Finally I found a way to chip from it successfully using my putter. The technique is useful regardless of the type of grass.

The shot is played with your putter when the ball is sitting a few inches into the second cut of rough. The ball can't be sitting down; the top three-quarters of the ball must be exposed. Play the ball back in your stance and place your hands ahead of the ball (*9-17*). Hit down on the ball slightly, finishing your follow-through just past the point of impact (*9-18*). The ball will jump and bound onto the green.

9-17, 9-18: When chipping from grass that is particularly wiry, try using your putter. The ball must be sitting up to try this shot. Simply hit down on the ball slightly, and it will pop over the tall grass and land on the fringe.

Chapter 10

WORKING
MIRACLES
FROM SAND

FEEL, TOUCH AND IMAGINATION can carry a golfer a long way. At the 1991 Ryder Cup Matches at Kiawah Island, S.C., no swing expert alive could have suggested an exact technique for playing the sand shot I hit on the 17th hole of my final-day singles match against Steven Richardson. My tee shot on the 210-yard, par-3 hole had plugged into a sand dune to the left of the green. The lie was uphill but the ball was below my feet. The sand was firm. It was one of the ugliest lies I'd ever seen. I stood 2 up at the time with only two holes left to play, and Steven had played a fine 1-iron tee shot to within 20 feet of the hole.

It looked like I was going to lose the hole. If Steven also won the 18th hole, that would mean a halved match and only half a point for the U.S. at a time when we needed a win and a full point. The team score was close, I had lost my matches the first two days and I desperately wanted to help the team.

My method for playing the shot was complicated to say the least. I chose my 60-degree sand wedge because I needed to hit the ball high enough to clear a ridge about 20 feet in front of me. From there it was another 40 feet to the hole, so I also needed plenty of forward momentum. I played the ball in the middle of my stance and opened my stance and the clubface. I took the club back outside and swung hard so the clubhead would penetrate the firm sand and slide under the ball. Because my lie was uphill, I wanted to slam the clubhead into the dune so it would stop just ahead of the ball and stay there. I just hit and hoped.

The ball carried the dune, landed on the green and started rolling. The sight of the shot coming off as I planned really fired me up. It made me lose control of my emotions. I ran up the dune and charged after the ball, coaxing it on until it rolled to a stop just 2½ feet short of the hole. Steven missed his putt and I holed my short one to halve the hole and win the match. Two hours later, the U.S. won the Ryder Cup Matches by a single point. It was one of the most exciting moments of my life.

Feel, touch and imagination had plenty to do with my hitting that sand shot close to the hole. To this day it rates as maybe the best shot I've ever hit in competition. But good technique played a role, too. Sand is one area where you must have good mechanics to perform well consistently.

Amateurs struggle merely to escape from bunkers, while good players try to hit the ball close to the hole. There's a huge gap in ability there, a gap that shouldn't exist. Once you understand the dynamics of sand play and how the clubhead must perform to make the ball pop out onto the green, it becomes one of the easiest shots in golf. By making just a few basic adjustments in your setup and swing, you can advance from being a poor player to a very good one.

Once you acquire good technique, sand shots are the most forgiving in the game. If on a standard shot you hit a couple of inches behind the ball, the ball will land short of the hole and roll up close for an easy putt. If you accidentally take less sand than you intended, that's fine, too—the ball will fly a little farther but will have more spin and stop close to the hole anyway. From a fat/thin standpoint, there's a nice margin for error.

OPEN ALIGNMENT PROMOTES
CORRECT SWING PATH

Two preswing adjustments will end your fear of sand immediately. The most common mistake amateurs make is aligning their feet and upper bodies square to the target at address and aligning the clubface square as well, as though they're playing a normal full-swing shot. But bunker shots are not played in a conventional manner. The square setup promotes a swing in which the clubhead approaches the ball from inside the line of play. The angle of approach is so shallow that the squared-off leading edge of the clubface digs into the sand and stops the clubhead from sliding under the ball.

Frustration magnifies the problem. After you flub a few shots by hitting behind the ball, your fear of leaving the ball in the bunker can cause you to try to pick it cleanly out of the sand. Now you err the other way, hitting the ball thin and flying it over the green. The square setup with your body and clubface simply leaves you with too little margin for error.

Photo 10-1 shows the correct setup. Your alignment must be *open*,

10-1: For the basic sand shot, you should align your feet to the left of the target line and open the clubface. This promotes an outside-to-inside swing path and a steep angle of approach, which gets the ball airborne quickly.

your feet, hips and shoulders aligned well to the left of the hole. That promotes an outside-to-inside swing in relation to the target line. The clubhead will approach the ball on a steeper angle and strike the sand just far enough behind the ball to allow it to pop out of the bunker.

SET CLUBFACE
OPEN, TOO

Virtually every bunker shot is played with the clubface open at address and at impact. The leading edge of the clubface should be aimed well to the right of your stance line but square to the target. When you open the clubface, you raise its leading edge, exposing more of the flange along the sole of the clubhead. The flange prevents the leading edge of the clubface from digging by allowing the clubhead to skid, or bounce, off the sand at impact. An open clubface also provides more loft, and that helps you hit the ball high and land it softly.

Every time you swing with an open setup, make sure you position the clubface open before finalizing your grip. Note in the photograph that my grip is normal although the clubface is open. Don't "fake" an open clubface by merely twisting your hands to the right.

FOOT SHIFT,
GRIP MUST MATCH UP

Depending on the type of sand you're playing from and the slope of the lie, your footing in bunkers can be precarious. You must preserve a solid stance at all costs. If your feet slide, you're in serious trouble. In fact, the very *thought* of sliding can break your concentration and cause you to hit the shot poorly, so it's important that you establish a solid, secure stance before you play the shot. Shift your feet into the sand far enough to reach the solid subsurface. Make a couple of practice swings—without touching the sand—to discern whether your footing will hold up during the swing itself.

The most important consideration of all is the relationship between your foot shift and your grip. If you twist your feet an inch below the surface, you must compensate by gripping down on the club an inch as well. If your feet shift downward but you maintain your normal grip, you'll have to change your posture so it's more upright, and that's wrong. Make the adjustment in your grip.

BREAK THE TEE
FOR OPTIMUM IMPACT

Your objective on standard greenside bunker shots isn't to gouge the ball out of the sand. You don't need a great deal of force nor do you need to dig the ball out. You merely want to slide the clubhead under the ball. A good image—and an effective practice drill—is to tee a ball in the bunker so the bottom of the ball is resting on the surface of the sand (*10-2*). Try to cut the tee in half through impact (*10-3*). It's almost

10-2: One of the best practice drills from sand is to tee the ball low and then play the shot. Your goal is to try to break the tee in half.

10-3: Note that my divot is deep enough to have dislodged the tee, yet shallow enough to show that I haven't penetrated the sand on too steep an angle.

impossible to cut the tee in half, but that should be the thought.

By trying to break the tee, you'll penetrate the clubhead about an inch below the ball, which is just about right on a uniform bunker surface. To dislodge the tee correctly, the clubhead will have to enter the sand a few inches behind the ball. If you hit too far behind the ball or hit the shot thin, the tee will remain embedded in the sand.

QUIET LEGS INSURE
PRECISE CONTACT

Just as on chips and pitches, you don't want much movement in your feet and legs when playing sand shots. It sets up a dangerous chain reaction—the legs move, your torso moves, your head moves. Ultimately, there's so much movement that your chances of striking the sand at the precise point are reduced considerably. The bunker swing is performed almost totally by your torso, shoulders, arms and hands.

Start by taking a wide stance, almost as wide as you would to hit a drive. The farther apart your legs are at address, the more difficult it becomes to move them during the swing. After you do that, there are two additional ways to keep your lower body quiet. The first is to angle your right knee in toward the target at address (*10-4*). Gary Player uses

10-4: Angling your right knee toward the target will restrict movement in your legs during the swing and reduce lateral movement as well. The basic sand shot is played primarily with your upper body.

10-5: A second method to keep your lower body quiet is to fan both feet out at address. This is an effective way to keep your body centered throughout the swing.

this technique on sand shots and he's been very successful with it. When your right knee is angled toward the target and left in that position *throughout the swing*, you won't drift laterally to your right on the backswing. Through impact, the position of your right leg, torso and head should remain the same as they were at address.

The second method is to fan your right foot out at address, so it mirrors the position of your left foot (*10-5*). Combine this right foot position by flexing at your knees, and it's very difficult to slide laterally to your right on the downswing. You'll stay centered over the ball and strike the shot cleanly.

DISTANCE:
FOLLOW-THROUGH IS KEY

There are different ways to control the distance the ball flies, most of them too sophisticated for even good players. I'm not a big believer in changing your ball position, choking down on the club unnecessarily or even changing the length of the swing. They all force you to make other adjustments and complicate what should be a simple process.

The difference between a 15-foot and a 30-foot bunker shot isn't much and should not be adjusted by your backswing. Try changing the length of your follow-through instead. When you need a short shot, "cut off" your follow-through so it finishes at waist-height (10-6). This softens your downswing so there isn't enough momentum to hit the ball

10-6: I'm playing a short shot and my follow-through shows it. Varying the length of your follow-through is easier than varying the length of your back-swing and is just as effective.

10-7—10-9: To play a low, running bunker shot, start by playing the ball back in your stance. Through impact, keep the club near the surface of the bunker. On the follow-through, pull your left elbow behind you.

a long way or carry you into a fuller finish. On longer bunker shots, make your follow-through longer. The mere thought of a longer follow-through will force you to make a more assertive downswing, and the ball will carry farther.

LOW AND HIGH
SAND SHOTS

To hit a low-flying shot from sand, start by placing the ball back in your stance (*10-7*). Take a standard backswing, but through impact (*10-8*) think of swinging the clubhead parallel to the surface of the sand, so the clubhead finishes low. Obtain a "chicken wing" look in your left arm by

pulling your left elbow behind you (10-9). The ball will come out low and run a long way. It's a good shot to own when you have lots of green to work with or you're hitting into the wind.

The high shot out of the bunker is much more difficult, especially when the ball is sitting down in the sand. If it's sitting down too much, it's best not to even try to hit the ball high. But if you have a clean lie, it's possible to hit the ball on a high trajectory with plenty of spin.

There are two preswing considerations. First, use your 60-degree sand wedge so you have maximum clubface loft and increase the loft even more by opening the clubface. Second, position the ball as far forward in your stance as you comfortably can (10-10). The backswing is normal, but through impact and into the follow-through (10-11, 10-12),

10-10—10-12: The technique for the high shot from sand is just the opposite of that for the low shot. Position the ball forward in your stance, and through impact keep your head down. On the follow-through, swing your hands as high as you can.

keep your head down until well after the ball is gone. Don't try to help the ball in the air. You want to deliver a descending blow, and keeping your head down will insure that you reach the ball comfortably, a difficult task because the ball is positioned forward in your stance.

Note the appearance of my follow-through in photo 10-12. My hands are high, the complete opposite of their appearance on the low shot. Try to copy that look. A high finish promotes a high ball flight.

UPHILL AND
DOWNHILL LIES

Uneven lies in bunkers require a cool head and important adjustments in your setup and swing. The key to the uphill lie is to set your shoulders parallel with the slope *(10-13)*, with about 80 percent of your weight on your right (downhill) foot. You need very solid footing with that right foot.

On the backswing, maintain the position of your right leg *(10-14)*

10-13—10-15: For an uphill lie, position your upper body perpendicular to the surface of the bunker at address. On the backswing, maintain the position of your right leg and shorten your turn. Through impact, swing the club parallel with the upslope.

and shorten your turn. You don't want lots of motion because gravity is trying to pull you down the slope. On the forward swing and through impact, swing the club parallel with the upslope, the club coming up very quickly after impact (*10-15*). Expect the ball to pop out high and land very softly.

The sand shot from a downslope is pretty tricky, too. The first thing you need to know is that the ball is going to run after landing, even if you have a good lie, so factor that into your planning.

As with the uphill lie, position your upper body perpendicular to the downslope at address (*10-16*), trying as much as possible to keep

your shoulders parallel with the bunker's surface. Shift most of your weight onto your left leg and fan your left foot outward so it can absorb the momentum of your body on the follow-through. Position the ball back in your stance as well. The tendency is to position the ball too far forward in an effort to help propel it into the air. If you do, you'll have a difficult time extending your arms far enough to reach the ball through impact. Obtain the necessary high trajectory by opening your stance as well as the clubface.

Keep your legs quiet on the backswing. On the downswing and through impact (10-17), avoid swinging the clubhead into the sand at a

10-16, 10-17: From a downhill lie, set your body perpendicular to the surface of the bunker, placing most of your weight on your left foot. Through impact, swing level with the downslope, so that the clubhead finishes low on the follow-through.

steep angle. Make a more level swing with the clubhead moving parallel with the bunker's surface.

THE FRIED-EGG
BUNKER LIE

No shot in golf looks as difficult, yet is as easy to execute, as the fried-egg lie in sand. The fried-egg results when a shot lands in the sand and remains right where it hit, the sand spreading out around it *(10-18)*. The ball is the yolk of the egg, the circle around it the white of the egg. The shot looks difficult because the lie creates a wall the clubhead must penetrate in order to reach the ball.

As difficult as the fried-egg lie looks, it isn't very hard to play successfully. In 95 percent of cases, you should at least get the ball on the green. Most of the time you should be able to get the ball to within one-putt distance of the hole.

The fried-egg lie poses one problem: The ball will roll after it lands because it's impossible to impart backspin on the shot. The amount of sand you're forced to take makes it impossible to strike the ball cleanly. So if you have a short bunker shot, accept that the ball will roll past the hole and don't try to invent a fancy way to make it stop. You can't do it.

Few golf shots require a hard swing, but the fried egg is an excep-

10-18—10-20: The conventional way to play the fried-egg bunker lie is to play the ball back in your stance, open the clubface and aim its leading edge at the rim of the sand. Hit down sharply with enough force to achieve a follow-through.

tion. You need lots of force because you have to hit a couple of inches behind the ball with a steep angle of approach. The clubhead has to have enough momentum to penetrate the sand deeply so it can displace the ball. It's no use trying to pick the ball cleanly out of its hole. If you hit the ball before the sand, the ball will fail to leave the bunker.

There are two ways to play the shot. The first is to play the ball

10-21, 10-22: When the sand is particularly firm or packed, address the ball with a square clubface so the leading edge will dig into the sand. Swing down hard on a steep angle. The digging action of the clubhead will shorten your follow-through.

back in your stance and open the clubface at address, aiming for the rim of the fried egg (*10-18, 10-19*). The ball-back position promotes a steep angle of approach on the downswing, which permits the clubhead to penetrate the sand. Despite the sharp downward hit, try to follow through after impact (*10-20*). If you attempt to finish the swing right at impact, the clubhead may not travel far enough forward to slide under the ball.

The second method is good for playing out of dense, packed sand. Square up the clubface at address (*10-21*) and don't align your body open as much. The very thing you try to avoid on standard bunker shots—the leading edge of the clubface digging into the sand—is what you want to have happen here. The clubhead will penetrate so deeply that the ball has to come out. The shot is played as a punch shot. Hit down hard behind the ball and don't follow through as far (*10-22*). The ball will come out lower, won't carry as far and will run like a wild thing after it hits the green.

TWO NEAT SHOTS

1. Ball plugged under lip

This can seem like a hopeless situation. You need quick elevation on the shot to clear the lip of the bunker, yet at the same time you're discouraged from hitting the ball high because the ball is buried. It's a true specialty shot that requires drastic changes in your club selection and swing technique.

Start by choosing your pitching wedge or 9-iron instead of your sand wedge. You want a club that digs into the sand rather than your sand wedge, which is designed to bounce off the sand. Next, position the ball back in your stance (*10-23*), so you'll hit down sharply just behind the ball. On the backswing keep your legs as motionless as possible and don't take the club back too far.

I liken the action on the downswing to chopping down a tree. You want to make an abrupt forceful swing and try to bury the clubhead under the lip of the bunker (*10-24*). You'll be surprised at how the ball reacts. It will pop into the air with plenty of elevation and land on the

10-23, 10-24: When your ball is plugged near the lip of the bunker, play the ball back in your stance to promote a sharp downward blow. The action on the downswing can be likened to chopping down a tree—your goal is to bury the clubhead under the lip of the bunker.

green softly. It won't have any backspin because the ball was plugged, but it won't run a long way, either.

2. How to play 'the hardest shot in golf'

There's only one shot in the entire game that doesn't discriminate according to handicap level. It is, of course, the 30- to 50-yard bunker shot, the bane of pros as well as amateurs. It's extremely demanding and difficult because you need to make a long swing, you can't take too much sand and you have to hit the ball with a club that would produce too much distance if you were in the fairway.

The first consideration is club selection. In a typical situation—a 40-yard shot with the ball sitting down slightly—go with an 8- or 9-iron, maybe even a pitching wedge. Every shot is different and only experience can tell you what club is best for a particular shot. From there, the technique is surprisingly similar to a standard sand shot. Align your feet, hips and shoulders open slightly, not quite as far as with a greenside bunker shot. Don't play the ball as far back as with a shorter shot; a hair to the right of center is about right (*10-25*). Open the clubface a bit to add loft.

Make sure you have good footing. You'll be making a slightly longer swing and you'll need a stable base. Make as long a backswing as you can without losing your balance or your footing (*10-26*). You don't need to swing super hard to pull the shot off—you already have plenty of club. Through impact, hit about an inch behind the ball (*10-27*), less than for a greenside bunker shot but enough to displace some sand. Then follow-through as fully as you can (*10-28*).

The results are surprising. The ball comes out fairly low due to the club you're using, but it has backspin due to the force of the swing and won't run as far as you might think.

If you have little confidence in your 8- or 9-iron, or so little practice time that you have trouble getting used to hitting the shot, there's a second option: Use your 56-degree sand wedge, playing the ball back in your stance so you decrease loft on the clubface. Don't position the clubface open as much at address, either, because that adds loft. Open it slightly and make a full swing. The ball will come out fairly low and behave much like it did with the 8- or 9-iron.

10-25—10-28 (clockwise from top left): To simplify the long bunker shot, play the ball just to the right of center in your stance and make as long a backswing as you can without losing your balance. Hit about an inch behind the ball—don't take too much sand—and make a full, extended follow-through.

Chapter 11

PUTTING IS
SHOTMAKING, TOO

In drawing up the initial outline for this book, there was some debate as to whether I should discuss putting at all. After all, you can't make a putt fade or draw. You can't hit the ball high and wouldn't want to. Wind is almost never a factor, your lie is almost always perfect and there's no jockeying around with club selection. In the context of actual shotmaking, putting seems to have so few variables, you could make the argument that it isn't worthy of discussion.

Two facts about putting convinced me otherwise. First, I estimate that putting is 40 percent of my game. Any advice on getting the ball from the tee to the green doesn't mean much if you can't putt well enough to score. The fact is, if you putt well, you'll almost never score badly. Conversely, a poor putter can, and will, shoot very high scores. It's a little ironic that a short putt can mean as much as a 250-yard drive, but that's golf.

Putting is the great equalizer in golf. Errant drives, sloppy iron shots, botched pitch shots and poor chips can be atoned for with a single good putt. There are many examples of smaller, less powerful golfers who have succeeded because of their short games, especially with the putter. Good putting unnerves opponents in match play, fills you with confidence in stroke play and gives you tremendous satisfaction.

Second, putting involves a great deal of creativity, imagination and diversity. Just as you make adjustments in your full swing to make the ball behave differently, alterations in your putting can drastically influence the way the ball rolls. The ability to read greens, discern grain, utilize strategy and impart a smooth roll to the ball qualifies putting as an art. No doubt about it, putting is shotmaking.

But putting is a science, too, and therein lies the promise for all golfers. Contrary to what you might have heard, good putters are made, not born. Improving your fundamentals, constructing a correct repeating stroke and understanding the factors that cause the ball to break on the greens, are physical aspects of putting that can be learned. So before going into the more advanced aspects of putting, a review of the fundamentals is necessary.

GRIP TAKES WRISTS
OUT OF STROKE

In the full swing, some wrist movement is necessary and desirable. With putting, it's just the opposite. You don't need the amount of club-head speed that cocking your wrists provides. The idea is to eliminate movement in your wrists as much as possible. On longer putts, minimal hinging of the wrists is acceptable, but on short and middle-range putts, your wrists shouldn't break at all. It signals deceleration and can disrupt precise clubface alignment.

I should point out that some of the more unusual putting grips we see today—the cross-handed grip is popular and Bernhard Langer braces his left hand by holding it with his right hand during the stroke—are designed to eliminate wrist hinging. The same principle applies with the extra-long putter, which is essentially swung with only one hand and no wrist movement at all.

I prefer a conventional putting grip with my right hand placed lower on the grip than my left. I think it affords maximum feel and I've had good success with it, so I've never been tempted to change. The most

11-1: The putting grip. By rotating your hands away from each other, you eliminate hinging of the wrists. On short- and medium-range putts, the wrists shouldn't hinge at all.

important facet of my grip is that I turn my left hand to the left so it's almost under the shaft *(11-1)*. This inhibits hinging of my left wrist. At the same time, I turn my right hand the same amount clockwise, or to the right. In a sense, my hands are "fighting" each other. But it's a friendly fight. Neither of my hands is inclined to hinge at the wrist during the stroke, and neither is likely to rotate excessively.

EYES OVER BALL
AT ADDRESS

Your perspective of the ball and the line of play as you look down at the ball at address is crucial. If your eyes are ahead of the ball, your view

11-2, 11-3: A good test to determine whether your eyes are directly over the ball at address is to drop a ball from the bridge of your nose. It should fall directly on top of the ball you are addressing.

will be misleading and you'll push or pull the putt. Your eyes should be directly over the ball or slightly behind the ball down the target line.

Try this test. Address the ball normally (*11-2*) and, keeping your head still, hold a second ball against the bridge of your nose. Now drop the ball (*11-3*). It should land directly on top of the ball you are addressing and displace it. If it drops slightly behind the ball and lands on top of your putter, fine. But you don't want the ball to drop up the target line from the one you're addressing.

This test will also determine whether your eyes are inside or outside of the target line. Ideally your eyes should be directly over the target line on every putt regardless of the length.

THE PATH TO
SOLID CONTACT

Solid club-ball contact in putting is underrated. If you hit the ball off-center, it can't roll the proper distance except by accident. The sweet spot of the putter—that dime-sized area that sends nice feedback up through the shaft to your hands at impact—is pretty elusive yet must be struck consistently if you're to putt well on a daily basis.

When I'm putting poorly or haven't played in a while, I like to stick tees in the green so they form a path to the hole (11-4). The path should be just wide enough to accommodate your putter. Practice hitting six-foot putts so the putter head swings through the path without striking the tees. The benefit is twofold. Not only will you learn to make

11-4: Practicing six-foot putts along a pathway formed by rows of tees promotes solid contact and a straight-back, straight-through stroke.

solid contact every time, but you'll train yourself to swing the putter on a consistent path.

HOLD CLUB LIGHTLY
THROUGHOUT STROKE

Some players prefer to hold the putter firmly, others like a grip pressure that's so light the putter nearly falls out of their hands. I recommend a fairly light grip pressure because it affords maximum sensitivity and touch, and also prevents your left wrist from breaking down as easily during the stroke. Holding the club tightly promotes hand action because the muscles in your arms are so tight they can't move freely.

11-5, 11-6: If the triangle formed by your shoulders and arms remains intact on the backswing and follow-through, it's a good bet it remained intact through impact. The relationship between the arms and shoulders should be constant at all stages of the stroke.

Once you grip the club lightly, keep that grip pressure constant throughout the stroke. You shouldn't increase the strength of your hold on the club on the forward swing because it will upset your rhythm and tempo. Grip the club lightly and keep it light until the ball is on its way to the hole.

MAINTAIN 'TRIANGLE'
AT ALL TIMES

Because your wrists don't hinge, something has to swing the putter back and through, and that task falls to the arms and shoulders. But you don't want excessive or faulty movement there, either. The arms and shoulders must perform together. At address, your shoulders and arms should form an inverted triangle, the shoulders acting as the base and your two arms as the sides. Try to keep the triangle intact on the backswing and follow-through (*11-5, 11-6*). If you swing with your arms only, you'll change the shape of the triangle.

The purpose of maintaining the triangle is consistency. By keeping the relationship between your arms and shoulders constant, you're more likely to return at impact to the position you established at address. In the precise world of putting, nothing less will do.

MAINTAIN THE 'Y,' TOO

Also important is the relationship between your arms and the clubshaft. If you observe your arms and the shaft at address, you'll see they form a "Y," with the arms forming the upper half of the letter and the shaft the vertical line that extends to the ground. During the backswing and even into the follow-through (*11-7, 11-8*), the Y should maintain its shape.

Again, the purpose of this alignment is consistency. If you break down by altering the position of your arms relative to each other or by cupping your left wrist on the downswing and follow-through, you'll have poor control over the speed and direction of the putt. Putt so you have that perfect "Y" position at impact every time.

Note that because the shaft is vertical at address, your hands are

11-7, 11-8: The relationship between your two arms and the clubshaft forms a rough "Y" at address. Your goal is to maintain the shape of the letter at all stages of the stroke.

directly over the ball. It's acceptable to position your hands slightly ahead of the ball, but never place them behind the ball. You'll increase the loft of the putter and encourage breaking down with the left wrist.

MAKE BACKSWING, FOLLOW-THROUGH SYMMETRICAL

One thing all good putters have is nice rhythm and tempo. The key is to keep the backswing and follow-through the same in length (*11-9*). If you make a short backswing and then a long follow-through, the forward stroke will have to be quick and abrupt to achieve that long finish. The sudden change in direction from the top of the backswing will be so sudden, there's no way you'll maintain a good feel for distance. On the other hand, if the backswing is long and your follow-through is short, you're decelerating through impact. That not only affects distance but the line as well.

The length of your backswing is a matter of personal preference and varies with the length of the putt. Paul Azinger has a very short backswing with the putter, while Ben Crenshaw's stroke is quite long. Mine is somewhere in the middle. What we have in common is that our respective swings are the same in length on either side of the ball. This allows us to accelerate the putter in a positive yet even manner on the forward swing.

11-9: An excellent way to build good rhythm and tempo during the stroke is to make your backswing and follow-through the same distance.

START PUTTER
DOWN TARGET LINE

Long putts mean a longer backswing, and at some point you're forced to swing the putter inside the target line. The "straight back, straight through" method works on shorter putts, but on longer putts you'd have to contort your arms to keep the putter moving along the target line. Still, try to swing the putter straight away from the ball for at least the first foot or so. That way you'll use your arms and shoulders to swing the putter while keeping your hips and legs dead still. Movement in the lower body makes it much more difficult to hit your putts solidly, affecting both distance and line. Your lower body should not move at all during the stroke.

Remember to maintain the triangle formed by the arms and shoulders and to keep the "Y" intact. That's the best way to keep the putterhead moving along the target line early in the stroke.

HEAD DOWN
THROUGH IMPACT

On short putts, there's a tendency to lift your head early in your eagerness to see where the ball went. It's a serious error because lifting your head can cause you to flinch with your upper body and throw your stroke out of kilter. Looking up also shows you're thinking about results when you should be concentrating on feel.

Keep your head down until well after the ball is gone, thinking the whole time only of how hard you're hitting the putt. Build self-discipline in practice—don't look up until the ball has come to rest. You'll hit your putts more solidly with better control of speed.

A DRILL FOR
BETTER LAG PUTTING

From my experience playing in pro-ams, lag putting rates as an across-the-board weakness among my amateur partners. Most of the three-putts I observe result from a player's inability to lag the long first putt close to the hole. I hate three-putting. All of the hard work you've put into getting the ball on the green is negated. I look at it as throwing away a stroke to par. In all but the most extreme cases, three-putting is careless and unnecessary. The chief cause is inattention to factors such as slope, grain in the greens and the overall speed of the putt.

On longer putts, distance is more important than line. You can push or pull a putt considerably—say, three feet—but if your putt has the right speed, you'll have a very makable second putt. But I see too many long putts finishing six feet short or long.

Long putts are "feel" putts. In addition to reading the green cor-

11-10: Speed control is critical on longer putts. To improve your touch, stroke a series of putts from 20 feet, keeping your head down until the ball stops rolling. See how accurately you can determine the distance each ball rolled.

rectly, you need to develop that intuitive sense for how hard to hit the putt. The next time you practice, lay down three balls about 20 feet from the hole and do your best to hole each one. Don't lift your head until the ball has come to rest (*11-10*). Before you look up, try to guess whether each ball was short or long of the hole. You might be surprised at how poor your judgment is at first, but with a little practice your long putts will come to rest much closer to the hole. You'll three-putt less often and hole your fair share.

HOW LONG IS
THREE FEET?

One of the worst habits among club-level amateurs—and I see it all the time—is that anything even close to the hole is considered "good" and they're encouraged to pick the ball up. In match play, this is understandable. Once a putt is conceded, go ahead and pick it up. But in casual play, the tendency is for amateurs to concede themselves putts that very well might be missed if they attempted to putt them.

Failure to hole short putts is disastrous in the long run. Under the heat of competition when you have to putt everything out, that "gimme" putt suddenly looks a lot longer. You won't have the confidence to put a firm, assertive stroke on it. It can be a shock to your psyche—not to mention your score.

Amateurs have a false sense for how long putts really are. Three feet in your mind may not seem very far, but I suggest you go to your putting green and lay your putter down at the hole. Your putter is in the neighborhood of 34 inches long, almost three feet. Now set a ball down at that distance. I'm betting that putt looks longer than the term "three feet" suggests.

Short putts are very "missable," even among top players. When I won the Honda Classic in 1992, I missed a one-foot putt on the 53rd hole of the tournament. Believe me, I was trying very hard to make it, and I just hit a bad putt. It reinforced my belief that a putt isn't good until it rattles the bottom of the hole. Practice those short putts because they mean as much or more than a long, straight drive.

HIT DOWN
ON YOUR PUTTS

Most of my beliefs about putting are pretty conventional. But there's one area where I depart from most of my colleagues. Most golfers try to make the putter move level through impact or even slightly upward. I believe in delivering a slightly descending blow.

Some experts will argue that hitting down on the ball drives it into the turf and causes it to hop. I've never found that to be the case. When I hit down ever so slightly on the ball, it seems to coast along the putting surface. Conversely, hitting up on the ball actually drives it into the green and causes it to bounce immediately. I'm the first to admit I don't know scientifically why hitting down on putts makes the ball roll better, but it works for me.

I'm not recommending that you hit down steeply on the ball. That would require that you swing the putter abruptly upward on the back-swing and that isn't wise because you'll tend to take the putter back outside the target line. On the backswing, keep the putter low to the ground. As you swing the putter forward, make it move downward so that it just brushes the grass at a point about an inch ahead of the ball.

BREAKING PUTTS:
FAVOR HIGH SIDE OF HOLE

The longer the putt, the more likely it is to curve (break) in one direction or the other due to a slope on the green. But regardless of the length of the putt, your strategy on all breaking putts should be the same: Favor the high side of the cup. There are two reasons for this. First, as the ball slows down it's affected more by the slope of the green and curves more as a result. As the putt dies, you want it to fall toward the hole. If you play the putt on the high side of the cup, it draws near-er the hole as it dies (11-11). On the other hand, the putt that approaches the low side of the hole the last four feet or so will roll far-ther from the hole as it slows down, leaving you with a testy second putt. You'll have fewer three-putt greens if you play the ball on the high side of the hole.

11-11: On breaking putts—longer ones especially—favor the high side of the hole. The idea is for the ball to draw closer to the hole as it slows down.

Second, playing the high side of the cup gives the ball more opportunities to go in. The ball that dies on the low side of the cup has no chance of going in, while the ball that's kept high on the sideslope can fall in the middle of the hole or even the far side of the hole.

By the way, this rule goes for chips, too!

LONG PUTTS:
DIE THE BALL AT THE HOLE

I hate the phrase "never up, never in," especially on long putts. It insinuates that the player wasn't bold or confident enough to strike the putt firmly. It's true that a putt left short of the hole didn't have a chance to fall. But experience has taught me that the ball that sailed five feet past the hole didn't go in either.

Your goal on long putts is to get down in two. Ideally you want the ball to reach the hole, but if it comes up two feet short, that's still a good putt. On shorter putts you have a realistic chance of making (15 feet is about the dividing line), you definitely should hit the ball firmly enough to roll about two feet beyond the hole. As you get closer, you definitely want to aim more toward the back of the hole and hit the ball firmly. But on longer putts, think more about getting down in two and plan your strategy accordingly.

LEFT-TO-RIGHT
BREAKING PUTTS

Most right-handed golfers consider putts that break from left-to-right more difficult than putts that break from right-to-left. In my opinion, they are slightly more difficult because you feel you have to pull your arms across your body on the forward stroke, almost as though you are deliberately pulling the putt. But a few simple adjustments in your set-up and stroke will make them as easy as the right-to-left breaker.

At address, set up more open than usual, your feet and shoulders aligned slightly farther to the left than seems necessary. Not only will you see the line better, you won't be tempted to pull your arms across your body on the forward swing. Instead of tucking your left arm behind you on the forward stroke so the putter swings to the left, think of pushing the putter out to the right, extending your right arm down the target line through impact (*11-12*).

To swing assertively, avoid steering the putter through impact and keep your head down well after the ball is gone.

11-12: The tendency on left-to-right breaking putts is to pull your arms nearer your body through impact. The solution is to extend your right arm through impact.

Another good tip: Avoid being "hole conscious," or too fixed on making the putt instead of starting the ball along the correct line. Practice left-to-right putts using an intermediate target such as a coin and practice rolling the ball over that spot.

Right-to-left breaking putts

These putts are easier for two reasons. First, amateurs tend to have more of them because their approach shots into greens end up on the right side of the green. Second, it's easier to make a putting stroke when your arms and hands are working away from your body, and that's the case with right-to-left breaking putts.

I have only one directive for these putts. After you survey the green and decide on the break, make sure you align the clubface squarely along the line you want the ball to start on *(11-13)* and make sure the ball rolls on that line. Don't "cheat" by aiming at the hole because you'll have to make an exaggerated inside-to-outside stroke to get the ball started on the proper line. Get a good read on the putt and trust what you see.

11-13: On right-to-left breaking putts, you want to avoid being too "hole conscious." After you've read the break, forget about the hole and think only of starting the ball on the correct line.

THE ART OF
READING GREENS

The direction the ball breaks is determined by gravity. From that standpoint, green-reading is a science. But it's an art, too, because the naked eye can't always discern local features that influence the ball's curvature on its path to the hole. If you learn some broad rules of thumb about reading greens, you'll seldom be fooled when you line up a putt.

Green-reading starts when you pull into the golf course parking lot. Not many amateurs know or appreciate that, but it's true. You can tell from standing by your car the following features that influence the ball on the greens. Ask yourself the following questions:

- *Where does the sun set?* Grass grows toward the setting sun. Generally, a putt that travels in a southwesterly direction—where the sun sets most of the year—will be faster than a putt traveling east. Some local features may override that rule; for instance, grass also tends to grow toward the nearest source of water, so if there's pond to the east and the putt is headed west, it will equal out.

  After you get out on the course, reading greens involves a lot more than what you see on the putting greens. When you prepare to putt, note the following:

- *Is there a pond or creek near the green?* All things being equal, a putt that appears to be flat will break toward water. This isn't just because the grain grows in that direction; generally greens are constructed to slope slightly toward a body of water because that's where they want water to drain when it rains.

- *Where's the highest peak in the vicinity?* When you're playing mountain courses, find out which peak is tallest. The ball will tend to break away from the highest peak.

- *What do the locals say?* When playing a strange course, ask one of the residents if there's a tendency for the ball to break in a certain direction. "The ball breaks toward Indio" (the lowest part of the valley) is a favorite saying at the Bob Hope Chrysler Classic in California, and there are many rules like it across the country.

• *Is the hole you're playing uphill?* After you've played to an elevated green, most putts that appear to be flat will break toward the front of the green.

A GRAIN-READING PRIMER

As short as the grass on greens is mowed, it's still long enough to affect the roll of the ball. Grass does not grow vertically. It grows toward the setting sun or toward water, and the nap formed by the growth pattern is called grain. Grain is more of a factor on Bermuda-grass greens than on bent grass, but all greens have at least some grain in them.

Because the grass is so short, it can be hard to determine the direction of the grain. A good method to find out is to stand in the middle of the green and take a look around. One half of the green will have a shiny appearance, while the other half will be noticeably darker. If you're putting into the shiny part, you're putting with the grain and the ball will coast along the grass without much interference. The putt will be faster. Putting into the grain is just the opposite. You'll have to hit the putt more firmly to get it to the hole.

If it's cloudy or overcast and the entire green seems to have the same complexion, examine the hole. One side of the cup will seem to be broken down, or eroded, more than the other. That part signifies the direction the grass is growing, the downgrain direction.

Note that when you putt sideways across the grain, the ball will break more sharply if it breaks in the direction the grass is growing. The slower the ball is rolling, the more the grain will affect it. When your ball breaks into the grain, the affect of the sideslope will be reduced.

TRUST YOUR
UPHILL READ

When it comes time to read a putt, don't take too much time. I go by the adage, "First sight is best sight."

In determining the line, the first impression you get from looking from behind the ball toward the hole is almost always the most accurate and will convey all of the information you need. If a putt looks straight, don't stare at the line for a long period of time trying to see if there's something you overlooked. Sooner or later, you'll invent a break that isn't there. As for speed, stand at the midway point between the ball and the hole and observe the entire length of the putt from a side perspective. Stand on the lower portion of the green, so you're looking uphill. That will give you the best indication of slope.

If you have plenty of time, you may want to observe the putt from the hole looking back toward the ball. But if your read from that view is contrary to what you saw from behind the ball, trust the read you got when looking uphill. It's almost always more accurate.

Chapter 12

GREAT ESCAPES

THERE ARE BAD LIES, then there are situations like the one I found myself in at the 1993 Ryder Cup at The Belfry in Sutton Coldfield, England. On the third hole of the Saturday afternoon four-ball matches, I drove my ball left underneath a tree. I crept under the branches and discovered that a normal backswing with my 3-wood wouldn't work. My practice swings kept colliding with the branches of the tree. I still had 220 yards to the hole and my partner, Jim Gallagher Jr., had to wonder if I was even going to advance the ball.

I took my time trying to figure out a way to hit the ball. I discovered that if I choked down on the club almost to the steel, my swing arc would be narrow enough for the clubhead to miss the branches. I played the ball in the middle of my stance and flexed my knees, which lowered my upper body and further insured my club wouldn't hit the tree. I made a relatively short backswing so I could maintain control of the club. I kept my lower body very still, swung as well as I could and hoped for the best.

The results surprised even me. The ball shot out low from under the tree due to my choking down on the club, landed well short of the green and rolled like crazy. It didn't stop until it rolled up on the green. I two-putted easily to halve the hole. Jim and I eventually defeated Mark James and Costantino Rocca 5 and 4.

My goal on the shot was more modest than the final result indicated. Your first goal on trouble shots is merely to hit the ball to a safe position. You don't want to compound the mistake that put you in trouble to begin with. All I was trying to do that day at The Belfry was advance the ball up the fairway. Had I swung all out, I might have hit the branches. And even if I had missed the branches, a big swing from that awkward position might have caused me to botch the shot. I might have turned a one-stroke error into a three-stroke error.

Any discussion of playing trouble shots starts with your mental approach. Trouble shots are almost always played under duress. You're upset because you hit a bad shot. You're concerned about the score you're going to make on the hole. There's the stress of playing a shot you haven't practiced, the concentration required to study your options and consider the percentage chances of pulling off the shot you want to play. Trouble shots demand imagination, composure, careful thinking, patience, self-discipline and excellent control of your swing.

Of course, they also require good technique. So far we've covered some of the more difficult lies you experience in golf—playing out of divots, tall grass, buried bunker lies and off sideslopes. To me those aren't trouble shots. Trouble means a ball on the edge of a cart path, behind a tree or playing with a restricted swing. Those are the shots I'll teach you.

There's something very satisfying about making a bogey when a double bogey or worse seemed likely. If one thing in golf is certain, it's that you'll hit bad shots, sometimes in seemingly impossible places. How you deal with those situations can make the difference between a good score and a poor one. More importantly, it can determine whether you have an enjoyable day or one that's miserable.

CONTROL YOUR
EMOTIONS

It's normal to get a little upset when you hit a poor shot into trouble. Golfers who blithely say they don't care about their score, that they're only there for the exercise, aren't being entirely honest—otherwise, they wouldn't keep score. The lousy shot that drifts into "tiger country" naturally provokes some disgust and anger. It's OK to be upset about a bad shot. But once you get to your ball, *calm down*. You've got golf to play. Anger clouds your thinking, warps your judgment and can cause you to make a careless swipe at the next shot—and then you'll know what real trouble is.

I have a little trick that works wonders at calming me down. When I hit a shot into trouble, I expect the worst. On the way to the ball, I imagine my ball is so snarled in tangled undergrowth that I'll be lucky to move it. When I get there and find that I can actually hit the ball—which you usually can—I'm almost grateful my lie isn't worse. It changes my mood for the better right away.

Even then, I take a deep breath and make certain I'm calm before I start examining my options. A cool head is a smart head.

GO WITH THE
'70 PERCENT RULE'

A typical trouble shot presents you with four options. You can (1) chip out to the fairway; (2) invoke the unplayable ball rule and proceed with a penalty; (3) hit the ball forward but short of where you'd hit the ball if you were playing from the fairway, or (4) attempt the all-out gamble toward the green. You now have a decision to make and, under stress, it's very easy to either bail out and play too cautiously or else bite off more than you can chew and compound your mistake.

I recommend a process that takes emotion out of the equation entirely and makes the decision for you. Start by considering the most difficult option, the heroic but risky play toward the green. If you were to play the shot 10 times, how many times would you pull it off successfully? Before giving yourself the green light to play the shot, the realistic answer should be, at least seven times out of 10. If you honestly don't believe you could successfully execute the shot 70 percent of the time, go to the second-hardest option. Is playing the ball toward the green but short of where you'd like it to be under normal circumstances still too ambitious? The "70 percent rule" answers that question. Proceed down the list until you believe you could pull off the shot 70 percent of the time.

There's one catch. You don't want an option that's too easy either, unless circumstances demand that you play ultra-conservatively. If you feel you could chip out to the fairway 10 times out of 10, you're underrating yourself. Proceed to the next-difficult option.

One factor should always be in the back of your mind. Are you playing match play or stroke play? Match play usually should prompt a decision to be more aggressive because if you fail to execute the shot you lose the hole but not the match. In stroke play, be more conservative. There's no limit to the score you can make on a hole, and if you get too greedy you can blow the tournament right there.

THE RESTRICTED
BACKSWING

When a tree or bush restricts your backswing, the problem is psychological as much as it is mechanical. The stress of worrying about hitting the tree distracts you from thinking of hitting the ball. You don't want to accidentally knock a branch off the tree in making a practice swing because that's a rules violation.

Your first task is to eliminate worry, and the answer lies in making your restricted swing more comfortable. Check how far back you can swing without striking the tree (12-1). Commit the length of swing to memory. Next, choke down on the club. That gives you more control of the club because you're making it lighter and easier to set at the "top" of your backswing. The last thing you need is a floppy top-of-backswing position, where the club extends so far back it collides with the tree.

Set up slightly open, your feet and shoulders aligned to the left of the target line. Because you're making a shorter backswing, you must

12-1—12-4 (clockwise from top left): When you're forced to make a restricted backswing, first determine how far back you can swing the club. Perform the backswing slowly with minimal wrist break. On the downswing, keep your head down and think only of hitting the ball solidly. Accelerate through the ball to a low finish.

make sure you turn your left hip aggressively at the beginning of the downswing. It's easier to do that from an open stance.

Swing the club back very slowly with minimal wrist cock (12-2). Your first move down from the top should be as deliberate as possible. If you "jump" on the shot, your arms, hands and shoulders will get out of sync and disrupt rhythm. Through impact (12-3), keep your head down and focus on hitting squarely into the back of the ball. Accelerate through the ball to a low finish (12-4). You'll be surprised at the power you achieve.

THE ONE-HANDED PUNCH

There are occasions when the ball stops near the trunk of a tree in a position where swinging at the ball normally isn't possible because the

12-5: To play the one-handed punch, your hand must lead the clubhead into the ball.

trunk intervenes. In that case, try hitting the ball one-handed. It isn't as hard as it looks—after you've practiced it a few times.

Stand upright with your back facing down the target line. Your ball should be positioned "back" in your stance—in this situation the ball should be played off the toe of your right foot. Set the club behind the ball so the clubhead is square to the target line and position your hand so it's nearer the target than the clubhead. This will help you hit down on the ball and get it airborne.

The tendency is to hit the ball fat, so when you swing one-handed, *make sure your hand leads the clubhead into the ball.* It's a punch shot, with the clubhead stabbing into the turf down the target line one inch ahead of the ball (*12-5*). The ball should pop out toward the target without much backspin.

THE LEFT-HANDED
SWING

The situation here is similar to the last, except that this time you need distance on the shot. You can't get at the ball right-handed, so all you do is hit the ball left-handed with the club turned upside down. Again this shot becomes fairly easy after you've tried it a few times.

At address, make sure the clubface is set square to the target. This is tricky because the angle of the clubface changes depending on the club you're using. A 9-iron, for example, will naturally be aimed farther to your right because of the clubface loft. Your club selection here is important. Don't use anything less than a 5-iron because it becomes too difficult to get the ball airborne.

The principles for the grip are the same except that the position of your hands relative to each other is reversed. Your left hand should rest lower on the club than your right hand. Position the ball back in your stance (*12-6*), as that makes it easier to hit the ball solidly. Now make several practice swings, noting where the clubhead strikes the turf.

The backswing should be a one-piece action with very little wrist cock and minimal leg movement (*12-7*). Perform the swing with your shoulders only. You want to simplify your swing by eliminating move-

12-6—12-8: To make a left-handed swing, position your left hand lower than your right, turn the club on its toe and play the ball back in your stance. Make a one-piece backswing, keeping your lower body as still as possible. To further encourage solid contact, keep your head down through impact.

ment in your hands and legs. Keep your backswing short. If you try to make a long swing to attain too much distance, you very well might whiff the shot. Keep your head down through impact (*12-8*), thinking of striking the ball squarely with the toe of the club. The ball will come out low and will go surprisingly far for making such a small swing.

BALL ON A
CART PATH

A cart path is an immovable obstruction and you are entitled to relief without penalty. But if you find yourself in a situation where a free drop at the nearest point of relief isn't practical because of a natural obstacle, it makes more sense to hit the ball off the path.

Because the path is paved, your spiked shoes can't penetrate it to provide good footing. At address, take a wide stance, as though hitting a

drive. The wider stance will inhibit a dramatic weight shift and leg movement, which would promote slipping. Also choke down on the club an inch for more club control.

Play the shot much like a fairway bunker shot, with a sweeping-type action through impact. Position the ball in the middle of your stance because you don't want to deliver a downward blow and strike the path. If you hit the path you might injure your wrists or damage your club. Hitting the ball "fat" in this case is also bad because the clubhead will bounce off the path and strike the ball thin.

Swing with your upper body alone, which further shortens your backswing (*12-9*) and discourages slipping. Through impact, think of striking the ball just below its equator. As with all trouble shots, keep your head down to insure clean club-ball contact (*12-10*).

12-9: *If you choose to play the ball off the cart path, play the ball in the center of your stance and make a shorter backswing to help maintain your footing.*

12-10: *Because precise contact is a must, keep your head down until well after the ball is gone.*

Chapter 13

A PERFECT FRAME OF MIND

FOR ALL OF MY ACCOMPLISHMENTS IN GOLF, I've had some setbacks, too. I went through a prolonged slump during 1988 and '89, when my swing just wouldn't produce quality shots consistently and I won only one tournament, the 1988 Texas Open. Talk about frustration. Before that, there was a stretch in my amateur days when I fought a bad temper and had very little patience. Since then I've made strategic errors that cost me tournaments, formed bad swing habits and experienced lapses in concentration at critical moments. When it comes to the mental side of golf, I've had my share of ups and downs.

I'll never forget the 1986 Masters, where I eagled the 15th hole in the final round to pull within one stroke of the lead. All I could think about as I walked to the 16th tee was that I actually had a good chance to fulfill one of my lifelong dreams. I was elated—too elated. I lost my composure and splashed my tee shot on the par-3 hole into the pond left of the green. Psychologically, it was a devastating experience. I remember sitting down on a bench near the tee and putting my face in my hands as though it were the end of the world.

I was a pretty good golfer in those years, but in no way was I a complete one. At the risk of sounding immodest, I know I wouldn't handle that situation at the Masters the same way today. I would calm myself down before hitting that tee shot so I could think more about how to execute the shot rather than how much it meant to me. And if by chance I hit the ball in the water, I wouldn't fall to pieces. I would immediately try to figure out a way to hit my next shot close to the hole so I would make only a bogey and then get back into contention with a birdie on the next hole.

As time passes, I become more and more convinced that improving your mental approach to golf is the real secret to becoming a good shotmaker and tough competitor. The mental side encompasses many areas, including practice habits, course management, preshot routine, relaxation, attitude and visualization. I don't believe the average golfer understands or appreciates the importance of those areas, nor do I think many golfers have the first idea about how to improve them. The typical amateur sees only the physical act of striking the ball.

I don't profess to know as much as a professional sports psychologist, but I've learned enough in my career about the nature of practicing and competing to dispense some practical information that will improve your mental approach and your shotmaking skills, too.

THE IMPORTANCE OF VISUALIZATION

What do you "see" in your mind when you stand over the ball? Most amateurs picture in their mind the shot they've decided to hit, but that image is vague. You may see the ball landing on the green, for instance, or the ball curving from left to right in the air. But visualizing the shot effectively is more comprehensive than that and can determine whether you make the type of swing that produces the desired ball flight. Your visualization skills will improve by doing four things.

- *Begin visualizing the moment you arrive at your ball.*
Examine the terrain between you and the green. You don't necessarily

have to fly the ball to the hole. I believe golf should be played point-to-point, and I don't care what route my ball takes to get to my target. If your lie is less than perfect, you may not be able to carry the ball all the way to the green. So inspect the terrain and how you can use it to your advantage. How firm is the turf? How does it slope? What club do you have to hit to make it land short of the green and bounce near the hole? The worst thing you can do—and I see it all the time—is to obtain the yardage and let it determine automatically what club you should hit. It's lazy, it isn't creative and it seldom is productive. By investigating various ways to get the ball to the green, you broaden your shotmaking alternatives and increase the chances of pulling off the shot.

Terrain isn't the only factor, of course. Which way is the wind blowing and how strong? What are the limitations of your lie? These factors not only determine your club selection, but the type of swing you should make.

• *See the shot from beginning to end.*
When you picture the shot, see it in its entirety. Relax and imagine the whole thing, from the moment the ball leaves the clubface to when it stops rolling. This takes practice, concentration and imagination, but anybody can do it. The reason you have to see the shot from beginning to end is that a lot of things can happen to the ball on its journey to the hole. It isn't enough to see the ball landing short of the green and bouncing forward from there. You have to take it one step further and ask, "How will it behave once it gets on the green?"

• *Envision every type of ball flight.*
There are four ways to hit a shot: high, low, fade and draw. Your first goal is to learn to hit the various combinations of these shots in practice. But the key to putting them to use on the course is to be able to visualize them. That's quite a different thing than mastering the mechanical skills that produce the various ball flights. If you're learning to hit a high fade, for instance, you won't feel comfortable hitting that shot on the course until you see it coming off clearly in your mind's

eye. It isn't merely a matter of training your body to hit the shot. You have to train your mind to hit the shot, too.

• *Translate the picture into action.*
As I've indicated several times in the earlier chapters, my whole premise to shotmaking is to let your setup dictate the shape of your swing. If you set up open, for example, you need only make your normal swing and the ball will fade. One reason I like that approach is that once I adapt my setup to suit the type of shot I want to make, my mind is free to "see" the shot clearly. I no longer need to devote all my thinking to swing mechanics.

Once you are over the ball, forget about your grip, your stance and of taking the club back a certain way. Think only of the picture you've formed of the shot. Somebody once asked Sam Snead how he hit a fade. His answer: "I think, 'fade.' " It's an example of how the mere vision of a shot secretly commanded his body to swing the club correctly without direct orders from his brain.

**PRACTICE
CREATIVELY**

For the most part, the type of "practice" I see on ranges isn't conducive to lasting improvement. High-handicappers seldom have a game plan for practicing. They machine-gun a bucket of balls using three or four clubs and then head for the first tee. It's more a glorified warm-up session than anything. The problem is that amateurs aren't sure how to practice productively. Here are some tips:

• *Don't hit the same shot twice in a row.*
On the course, you have only one chance to hit a shot successfully—unless you hit the ball out-of-bounds. Adopt that mindset on the practice range. Hitting 10 consecutive draws isn't very productive because only your first attempt reveals whether you are making the type of swing you need to make the ball curve from right to left. Mix up your practice. If you have a 7-iron, hit the first shot high, the next one low.

Fade the next and draw the next one after that. The variety will force you to concentrate on your setup and keep your mind fresh. Every shot will be a challenge and you'll gain a quicker understanding of the feel and mechanics required to work the ball efficiently.

• *See the "hole," not the practice range.*
Looking out at the vast expanse of a practice range, it's easy to choose a rather vague target and just whale away. I even see many amateurs raking another practice ball toward them before the shot they just hit even hits the ground. Be more specific about your target. Envision a green or a fairway down the range and be more precise about trying to hit it. Be especially cognizant of distance. Yardage signs aren't known for being exact, so don't pay too much attention to them. Pay more attention to how far one shot flies in relation to another.

• *Hit lots of "ridiculous" shots.*
If you want to improve your feel for hitting fades and draws quickly, practice hitting shots you wouldn't dream of hitting under normal circumstances on the golf course. Instead of trying to hit a 10-yard draw with your 5-iron, try to hit a 20-yard draw, exaggerating your setup to produce a sweeping hook. Hit 150-yard shots with your driver, head-high punch shots with your 4-wood, huge slices with your 2-iron. It's great for playing trouble shots, learning to alter your setup and trust it. It's also a lot of fun.

• *Make your practice interesting.*
Hitting balls can be drudgery and motivation is perhaps the biggest obstacle to practicing regularly. The key is to make your practice fun. It helps to practice with a friend because you can help each other and instill a friendly competitive spirit. Try playing practice games against each other. One of the best is "call shot," a game I play with my caddie, Eric Schwarz, all the time. The game is played to 10. One of the players names a type of shot to hit, say a low fade, and both players attempt the shot. Closest to the target wins a point. The low fade (or any shot you call) must be properly executed. The player who wins the point

gets the "honor" and the right to name the next type of shot. The only rule is that you can't name the same shot twice in a row.

The games don't have to be limited to the practice range. A good on-course game is "worst ball." The players hit two drives each and have to play their worst. You play two shots from that point, again having to play your worst one. Worst ball is a tough game. Par on a hole is a great score and birdies are very rare. It teaches you course management, which is the ability to keep the ball in play and play the holes the way they were designed. Before long, you'll see the wisdom of choosing a 3-wood off the tee of tight driving holes and aiming for the middle of the greens instead of going straight at a flagstick just over a bunker.

A great game for developing your shotmaking skills is a two-club challenge. Select any two clubs you like and play a nine-hole match against a friend. It's a thinking man's game. If you choose to carry a 5-iron and 9-iron, you'll find that to score well you have to play strategically, aiming the 5-iron to a spot where you have optimum yardage for the approach with the 9-iron. Conversely, if you're 230 yards from the hole, you want to hit your next shot with the 9-iron instead of the 5-iron because a short punch with the 9-iron will leave you with 130 yards or so to the green—perfect distance for another 9-iron shot. You'll want to avoid bunkers at all costs, of course, because you don't have a sand wedge. The two-club challenge will teach you to hit partial shots and to hit the ball higher and lower than normal.

STAY ON
AN EVEN KEEL

I explained in Chapter 12 on trouble shots how a bad temper can cause you to turn a bogey into a double bogey or worse. The flip side to losing your temper is getting too excited over something good, and the results can be just as disastrous. That eagle I made at the 1986 Masters was a good example. I was so ecstatic over getting into contention that the adrenaline began pouring through me. My mind was racing and all I could think about was the possibility of winning the tournament. I really lost my composure.

When something positive happens, be it a long putt, a holed shot from the fairway or simply a stretch of error-free play that has you on track to shoot your best score ever, the challenge is to subdue your emotions so you can still function normally. Handled intelligently, a little adrenaline can help you. You can hit the ball farther, your senses are razor-sharp and your confidence soars. But it's important to stay in the present tense, to think about the shot you have to play rather than the outcome two or three holes ahead.

HOW TO
HANDLE PRESSURE

I've come to enjoy intense pressure. I'm always curious to see how I'll react to the stress, how well I'll respond to the test before me and what I'll learn from each experience. To a great extent, of course, I've learned how to handle stress simply by being under the gun so often. The amateur who is subjected to extreme pressure only once a year or so faces a more difficult task because he's treading on unfamiliar ground.

Pressure affects each person differently. In any case, it can have a huge, debilitating effect on shotmaking. Creating shots requires imagination and an uncluttered mind. Pressure has a way of clouding your thinking so you can't visualize the shot properly. It also tightens you physically, so you have a hard time making the type of swing necessary to play a special type of shot.

Unfortunately, there are no shortcuts to handling pressure. The most common response to pressure is fear of failure. Nobody wants to look foolish in front of a crowd of people and nobody wants to carry around the stigma of choking under pressure. The fear of failure causes you to focus on where not to hit the ball rather than on hitting the ball aggressively toward your target. If you are unfamiliar with pressure, you don't see the fairways and greens. Suddenly the bunkers and ponds seem larger, like giant traps waiting to snare your ball. A pattern of negative thinking sets in, and if you think you will fail, it's almost certain that you will fail.

From a mechanical standpoint, the solution to this type of pressure is to go with your tried and true shot whenever possible. You have to try to hit the shot you know you can count on. If the shot calls for a draw and you're more comfortable with a fade, go ahead and hit the fade. *Play within your capabilities.*

The other type of fear is a bit more unusual. It's the fear of success. With success comes expectations from others and a reputation you have to protect. Some people fear the consequences of success. They think, "If I beat the club champion, that means I have to play like the best golfer in the club. I'm not sure I want that kind of day-to-day pressure."

In that case, remind yourself that the expectations of others don't mean a thing. The only standards that matter are your own. In my case, seeing my name in newspapers, books and magazine articles, while flattering, has no bearing on how I view myself or my golf game. Worrying about what other people think is a recipe for underachievement. You have to have your own standards and work within them. Ignore other people's thoughts about what you should be doing.

Although there is no way you can remove pressure altogether, there are several techniques that will help you function better when the heat is on:

• *Relax your shoulders.*
Pressure creates physical tension. In most cases, tension sets in around your neck and shoulders, so the shoulders actually are raised. This tightness affects your ability to turn, shortening your swing and quickening it. Concentrate on keeping your shoulders as loose as possible. Just before you step up to the ball, tighten your shoulders and arms even more, then slowly relax them. You should feel your shoulders sag as you do this.

• *Breathe deeply.*
This tip may sound like a no-brainer, but under pressure it's easy to forget. Just before you begin your preshot routine, take a deep breath, inhaling through your nose and exhaling from your mouth. This not only supplies much-needed oxygen to your bloodstream, it has a calming effect as well.

• *Do everything slowly.*

There's a tendency under pressure to walk faster, swing faster and think faster. Make a conscious effort to slow everything down. Walk a bit more slowly to your ball and take smaller steps. When you arrive at the ball, take your time. I'm not promoting slow play. In fact, these thoughts probably will slow you down to normal speed. Most important is to swing slowly. One of your last thoughts as you stand over the ball should be to swing rhythmically with a smooth tempo.

• *Seek out pressure situations.*

If you're serious about playing better in competition, try to get in as many realistic pressure situations as possible. Play more matches with your friends and acquaintances and see how you respond under pressure. Chances are you'll find a pattern to your poor shots under pressure. You'll know what to expect and can anticipate and make allowances for your worst tendencies.

• *Between shots, get your mind off the subject.*

There probably is one aspect of your swing or the competition that is a major source of nervousness. Maybe it was a poor shot you hit a few holes back. Will the same swing flaw recur now? Or maybe it's the thought of winning the match or the tournament. In any case, don't dwell on it during your "down time" between shots because you'll just intensify your anxiety. Think of something else. Talk about something totally unrelated to the matter at hand.

The idea is to concentrate for short periods of time. Years ago, I used to concentrate furiously from the moment I teed off until I walked off the 18th green. The rounds used to leave me exhausted. Eventually I learned to concentrate in short bursts. A good model is Lee Trevino. Lee talks up a storm between shots, laughs and jokes a lot. But when it's time to hit the shot, he concentrates as fully and intently as any golfer in history.

HOW TO PLAY
THE HOLE YOU HATE

There's probably a hole at your home course—maybe several holes—that feels uncomfortable to you. Maybe you like to fade the ball and the hole bends from right to left, favoring a draw. Perhaps the green demands a high shot and you're a low-ball hitter. In any case, if you don't like the design of a hole, you probably won't play it well because your negative mindset subtly affects the way you play it.

That's how the 16th hole at Augusta National used to be for me. What I haven't told you is that I not only hit my tee shot in the water there on Sunday, I hit it in the water on Saturday, too. I disliked that hole intensely and I let it get the best of me.

The following year I was determined to play the 16th better. In the practice rounds I hit more than one shot to the green. I imagined the hole being in four locations and I played a shot at each one. I played that hole to death until I was familiar with every dip and swale. My preparation paid off. I played the hole in two under par in 1987. And in 1992 I made a hole-in-one there.

The key then is to play the hole until you find a way, any way, to play it well. It may mean taking one club more than normal and swinging easier. It may mean aiming for the fat part of the green and accepting a two-putt for par. Form a game plan, *be decisive and stick to your strategy*. Never change your strategy because once you do, you'll feel uncomfortable all over again.

THE IMPORTANCE OF
A PRESHOT ROUTINE

One of the goals in golf is to construct a dependable, repeating swing. The shotmaking process embodies several elements and I believe that the more efficiently you can repeat them, the better chance you'll have of making the same swing every time. A comfortable, familiar preshot routine is a critical first step in the process.

If you prepare for each shot differently, you won't develop the same inner rhythm and thought processes. Under pressure, your concentration will be easily shattered. You might align your feet and shoulders improperly. You may hit the shot too quickly. You might feel uncomfortable. Without a sense of order in your preshot routine, you'll decrease your chances of making that repeating swing.

The ingredients of a good preshot routine vary from player to player. Here's the one I'm using now, which I formulated with Dr. Coop:

Step 1: Select an intermediate target. After I determine my yardage and decide which club I want to hit, I find an object between my ball and the target about 10 yards in front of my ball. It may be an old divot or a discoloration in the turf. But I concentrate on that spot.

Step 2: Make a practice swing. As I visualize the type of shot I want to hit, I rehearse the type of swing that will produce the desired ball flight. There is no predetermined number of practice swings. I might make as few as one or as many as five. I practice swings until I feel comfortable.

Step 3: Ignite the trigger mechanism. You need a small signal that it's time to begin the procedure of hitting the shot. For me, it's a tug on the left pocket of my pants. Some golfers tug the bill of their cap, others twirl the club in their hands. It's a cue that it's time to get things under way.

Step 4: Step into place with the right foot. Do this at the same time you seat the club behind the ball, aiming the clubface at the target.

Step 5: Step into place with the left foot. The placing of your left foot determines ball position. As I settle my left foot into place, I rock back and forth from foot to foot, "feeling" my way into my address position and making tiny adjustments in my ball position. This is the final adjustment of the address procedure.

Step 6: Make a forward press. Some golfers shift their hands a bit toward the target. Some golfers tap the ball of their foot lightly on the ground. Others swivel their head a bit to the left. I like to make a small movement with my left hip. The purpose of the forward press is to establish rhythm and set the swing into motion.

The preshot routine you select doesn't have to remain fixed for life. In fact, I find it useful to make some small alteration in my preshot routine every three months or so, just to keep it fresh and crisp. Usually it's a change in my trigger mechanism. In fact, by the time this book hits the stores, I may no longer be tugging at my left pocket.

FINALLY,
HAVE FUN

The golfer who plays the best is the one who enjoys golf the most. The question is: Which comes first, enjoying the game or playing it well? I believe the golfer who drives into the parking lot anticipating a good time can't help but play well most of the time. There's something to be said for optimism and a carefree spirit.

If I weren't a professional golfer, chances are I'd play all the time anyway. Golf is the greatest game in the world. It's the most challenging, the most rewarding and the most exhilarating. The wide variety of people I've met, the friendships I've made, the hundreds of beautiful golf courses and cities I've visited worldwide, the opportunity it has given me to make a good living for my family; these things combined have made me happy to have chosen the game for my life's work.

I hope you take my advice seriously and work on your game as your free time allows. Bobby Jones once said that golf is much more fun when it is played well, and I can attest to that. And even if you don't become a scratch player, there's still considerable happiness and satisfaction to be gained by improving.

That's why I keep playing golf. A voice inside my head tells me I'm still improving.